Cold War II

Jensen Cox

Published by Miller, 2023.

COLD WAR II

First edition. May 31, 2023.

Copyright © 2023 Jensen Cox.

ISBN: 979-8223567738

Written by Jensen Cox.

Table of Contents

Cold War II

Jensen Cox

The book

———

And Cold War II began. It will be profoundly different from the first. Many things will change for all of us, in the challenge between America and China no one will be able to remain neutral. The economy and finance, science and technology, political values and culture, every terrain will be affected by the new conflict. We must stop talking about globalization as if it were irreversible: its retreat has begun. Fifteen years after his best-sellers *The Chinese Century* and *The Empire of Cindia* , Jensen Cox returns to attack stereotypes, forces us to review clichés, opens our eyes. The world has changed much more than Westerners realize.

The sunset of the American century and the possible transition to the Chinese century are forging ahead. We got distracted while China underwent a shocking metamorphosis: it has overtaken us in the most advanced technologies, aims for supremacy in artificial intelligence and digital innovations. It is at the forefront of modernity but remains an authoritarian regime, even tougher and more nationalist under Xi Jinping. Combining Confucius and meritocracy, she theorizes the superiority of her political model, and the crisis of the liberal democracies seems to prove her right. Italy is a land of conquest for the New Silk Roads. A historic Chinese invasion is underway in Africa.

Two empires, one declining and the other on the rise, slide towards confrontation. America has convinced itself that, "it is now or never", China must be stopped. Will those in the middle, like the Europeans, be crushed? No one is equipped to face the coming storm. Not even the leaders of the two superpowers have a clear idea about the next installments of this story, about the final point of arrival. They set in motion forces that they themselves will not be able to fully master.

A few years ago, the two superpowers seemed to have become almost one, such was the symbiosis between the world's factory (Chinese) and its outlet market (American). That era has ended and will not return. What many experts considered impossible is happening. The tariffs were only the accelerator of a divorce that will change the maps of our future. The showdown plummets at all levels. This book is a guide and a survival manual in the new world that awaits us.

Introduction

The sunset of the American century and the possible transition to the Chinese century forge ahead, the scenario becomes current and happens in the most shocking way. It's turbulent, traumatic. Two empires, one in decline and the other on the rise, are speeding up the showdown. Who is in the middle - like the Europeans - will end up like an earthenware pot? None of us are equipped to face the coming storm. Not even the leaders in command of the two superpowers have a clear idea on the dynamics of the challenge, on the next episodes of this story, on the final point of arrival. They set in motion forces that they themselves will not be able to fully master. It's a new world, which in a short time is erasing the rules set in the previous era. We need to understand this, it's a matter of survival.

The Cold War officially ended 30 years ago. But the US-USSR thaw had begun even before the fall of the Berlin Wall. For this reason we have a faint memory of the acute tensions between the two blocs, when nuclear war was a real danger, crossing the "iron curtain" was a feat (above all from the communist world towards the West); there were ideological wars and "witch hunts" on both sides.

Then there are the many young people born after that fateful 1989. For them the concept of the Cold War is abstract; assuming they've heard of it. It's time to rediscover it, updated to the new reality. The new cold war is beginning, but it will be profoundly different from the first. Many things will change for all of us, in this challenge between America and China no one will be able to remain truly neutral. The economy and finance, science and technology, political values and culture, every terrain will be affected by the new conflict. It will be necessary to stop talking about globalization as if it were an irreversible phenomenon: its retreat has already begun. Perhaps it is more reasonable to say that we are entering a different chapter of globalization, with more visible or invisible barriers.

Do you remember the term «Chimeric»? The neologism was coined by historian Niall Ferguson and economist Moritz Schularick, merging the words "China + America". It only happened in 2007. In the same period, geopolitical gurus were talking about the birth of a G2 that would replace the various G7 and G20; the world seemed to be moving towards a two-way directory, in which the United States and the People's Republic of China would make the big decisions together. Chimerica and G2 remind us of an era in which the two superpowers seemed to have become almost one, at least in terms of economy and finance: such was the complementarity of roles, the symbiosis between the (Chinese) world factory and its (American) market. That era has ended and will never come back. What many experts considered impossible is happening at breakneck speed. Donald Trump's tariffs must not obsess us: they were only the latest episode of a crisis, the brutal way in which an American leader shouted to the world that "the emperor is naked". The trade war, which can experience temporary truces or compromises, has only been the accelerator of a divorce that will change the maps of our future, and will have consequences for Europe.

Trump may be impeached or lose the election in 2020, but the Democrats who challenge him have become even tougher on Beijing than he is. The showdown is fast approaching, at all levels: the major US multinationals are reviewing their Chinese plans and their dependence on that country. When a digital giant like Google decides to deny its software to Huawei, the Chinese telephony champion, it is because it prefers to lose a large customer rather than expose itself to its technological espionage... and to the sanctions of the federal government in Washington. Cases like this are multiplying even if it's not a stampede yet. American groups such as Apple Boeing and General Motors (or Germans such as Siemens, Audi-Volkswagen) have done fantastic business in China: first they produced there for years at low cost, then they discovered a new customer, the vast Asian middle class; today they reluctantly reduce their dependence on that market and that "factory".

Everyone is looking for alternatives, escape routes, strategic retreat plans. It is the end of a thirty-year piece of globalization history. And with it a certain world order was also waning: as long as the conviction prevailed between Washington and Beijing that they had a lot to gain in the division of roles, their relationship generated stability. That symbiosis, made up of interpenetration and mutual benefit, seemed irreversible. Today the rest of the world – including the Made in Italy sectors that have had success in China and the circles of the Italian economy attracted by Xi Jinping's New Silk Roads – must know that the rules of the global game are changing. We will all be involved in the great challenge.

Don't focus on Trump. The character is unpredictable, this is part of his negotiating tactic, we know that. It may surprise us to attempt a sudden understanding with Xi Jinping to stop the escalation of protectionism. But beyond the drama, nothing will ever be the same again. The entire American establishment – including a section of capitalism, the technocratic elites, the old democratic establishment and of course the Pentagon military – has revised its optimism about the Chinese opportunity. In part, it is Beijing's success that has caused this cooling. The old division of labor between an advanced economy and an emerging one envisaged relocations to a country with low labor costs, which also re-exported many US-branded products to the American market. Imbalances in the trade balance, or the dismantling of the American working class, worried neither the capitalists of Silicon Valley nor the bankers of Wall Street. China's strategy has ensured rich profits for everyone. But Xi Jinping's China is reaping the fruits of a great emancipatory project. She was good and ruthless at the same time; its people, its entrepreneurs, its rulers have resurrected ancient traditions that had made the Celestial Empire the richest power on the planet; they unleashed talent and determination, cunning and cynicism; they beat us at our own game, sometimes by cheating.

This China is less and less emerging and more and more emerged; in many areas the pupil has surpassed the master; aims for world supremacy in advanced technologies. That Amazon is forced to close its Chinese operations is the consequence of the fact that Beijing has cultivated (by legal and illicit means) national champions who are scorched earth around many foreign companies; it has also been able to nurture a hyper-competitive, aggressive, innovative local entrepreneurship. Added to this is the awareness of the Pentagon and US intelligence that Beijing is forging ahead even in the political-military run-up.

Xi is the first leader who proclaims *urbi et orbi* the superiority of his authoritarian model over our liberal democracies.

The scenario of the "Thucydides trap" (the Athens-Sparta rivalry that led to the Peloponnesian War) needs to be studied more and more carefully. A professor at the Harvard Kennedy School, an expert in military history and strategy, Graham Allison, sensed this in 2015. His essay *Destined for War. Can America and China Escape the Thucydides Trap?* (Fazi Editore, 2018) was carefully studied in Beijing, and Xi Jinping mentioned it in his first meeting with Trump. The use made by the Chinese is evident: they tell us Westerners, and America in particular, that we must not fall into the trap of other powers, those who in the past tried to block the rise of a rival by any means, including war. But the trap can be triggered in many ways. The behavior of Chinese leaders is helping to fuel fear, distrust and resentment in the West. The idea that "we need to stop them before it's too late" has also made inroads in environments very far from Trumpian sovereignty and protectionism.

In the long run, prophecies are often denied, history loves surprises. But we must prepare for a series of armed truces, ephemeral compromises in which America and China will study their adversary to prepare new offensives. We should use breaks to prepare for the worst. Personally, having contributed to explaining the "new China" to Italians when its power was still in its infancy (my books *The Chinese Century* , *The Empire of Cindia* and *The Shadow of Mao* came out between 2005 and 2007), I feel the need to update that analysis. Starting from a balance sheet of all the changes that have occurred since my move from Beijing to New York.

Five days of blue sky in Beijing: it is one of the first surprises – this one decidedly positive – that welcome me on my return. Ten years ago I ended my Chinese experience. I had inaugurated the first «Republic» correspondence office in Beijing in July 2004, I would stay there until I moved to New York in July 2009. Since then I have returned there regularly, about once a year. Often as an envoy following a US president, Barack Obama or Donald Trump, to follow a bilateral summit or super-summits like the G20. Other times on vacation to see my three adopted children. So I've never really pulled the plug, the attention towards China has remained constant. But anniversaries make you more sensitive to changes; they force you to make budgets. So this last visit – all private, a family reunion – forced me to measure the distance travelled. Huge. Yes, China has changed a lot in these ten years. We didn't realize it enough. Perhaps also because this country has closed itself off to information, has erected higher barriers that hinder the circulation of news and ideas in both directions. They suffer censorship at home, but we too have unknowingly suffered from a certain scarcity of information.

Retreating pollution is a great thing. My five days of blue sky could be a coincidence due to particularly fortunate weather conditions, with beneficial winds from the right direction that sweep away the smog. But July is a difficult month, because the temperature rises a lot, I remember the oppressive, unlivable summers, with the heat and the pollution that merged into a toxic mixture that caught your throat. The summer of 2008 was an exception due to the Olympics: a turning point event, which was to consecrate the new international status of the Chinese superpower in the eyes of the whole world. In order not to disturb that celebration in any way, the authorities – Hu Jintao was then president – took more than drastic, draconian measures: many weeks before the opening of the Games they closed all the factories in a vast urban perimeter and also in the outskirts enlarged; private cars were banned or subjected to severe restrictions; the public offices forced part of the staff on holiday to reduce the resident population and therefore energy consumption. All these measures proved to be effective: if you stop the economy you cut down on pollution. But today many Chinese and foreign friends who live in Beijing confirm a new reality for me. It is no longer only on the occasion of major international events that the "blue skies" operation is triggered. Pollution is steadily decreasing. Really fantastic news, which I would not have expected ten years ago: not so quickly.

This is a textbook case where the methods of an authoritarian regime work. A dear Chinese friend – in some cases I avoid mentioning names, you'll understand why – tells me his personal version. He is a small businessman, he produces and maintains solar panels, therefore an environmentalist business. However, since it is classified as a "factory", his company was also affected by the government edict: it had to move very far from the capital. He argues that by doing so the government is simply transferring pollution from one region to another. But the feeling is that many things are moving in the right direction. On an anecdotal level, I note an invasion of Tesla and other electric cars on the streets of Beijing, encouraged by the "green plate" which exempts them from shifts (other cars cannot circulate on certain days of the week, in rotation). No yellow vests to protest against these measures, on the streets of the Chinese capital! At a macro level: through renewable sources alone, China now produces more clean electricity than Germany generates with all sources, including fossil energies.

China's leap forward in this decade is even more spectacular in another field: the mastery of digital technologies. I felt like a troglodyte, entering the shops with my little piece of plastic: the credit card is prehistoric, it is pathetically outdated. By now the average Chinese uses a single smartphone app, for example associated with the Weixin messaging system (called WeChat in English, it replaces our WhatsApp which is forbidden in China), for an infinite series of functions in their daily life. When paying, in a shop or restaurant, but also at the valet and in many public services such as transport, just open the Weixin screen with the QR, cryptogram or square barcode. The QR is seen by the merchant's optical reader and authorizes the payment. The volume of smartphone payments in China is estimated to be one hundred times that of the United States. A hundredfold, yes. When I left Beijing we were still in the "run-up" phase, today the student has surpassed the master. In many ways the future is today's China, we are the past.

The leap forward in modernity, when coupled with rising nationalism, has more surprises in store for me. In «my» China of ten years ago it was a status symbol of the young upper-middle urban class to go shopping in Carrefour hypermarkets or Ikea: a way to conform to the West and a sign of xenophilia in consumption, to distinguish oneself from the provincial and rural people. Today Carrefour is in crisis, supplanted by many agile Chinese start-ups that offer home delivery and save you from traffic jams. From *car-sharing* to online commerce, all Silicon Valley forerunners are in trouble. Amazon closes its doors because it is vanquished by Alibaba; Uber can't compete with its Chinese *car-sharing* (or *bike-sharing*) counterparts. Behind this retreat of Western companies there is also a good dose of protectionism, covert or overt. But not everything boils down to discriminatory government action. The growth of a local entrepreneurial fabric whose capabilities Westerners have underestimated, too convinced of being the first in their class, also weighs heavily. Finally, there is a spontaneous nationalism of consumers. In the last year of my stay in Beijing, the inauguration of the first Apple Store made headlines, the young people of the middle class lined up to get inside. Today, Apple iPhones have slipped to fifth place among the best-selling brands. Made in China, for many Chinese, has become synonymous with an even more advanced quality than ours. Something similar happened in Japan in the 1970s, in South Korea, Singapore and Taiwan in the 1980s. Even then, someone warned that Asia would once again be the center of the world and we the periphery. But today a nation of 1.4 billion inhabitants is overtaking the West. And with an authoritarian-nationalist regime. It's much more complicated.

It is a chic, refined and cosmopolitan Beijing that welcomes me inside Page One, the beautiful bookshop opened in an elegantly designed room. The shelves are also crowded with American and English titles. The audience that surrounds me, in dress and manner, could be in Manhattan or Tribeca or Soho; or in London, Berlin or Paris. And yet... The choice of titles in foreign languages is very rich for modern and contemporary classical literature; very limited instead for non-fiction. Nothing is sold that would be inconvenient or irritating to the regime. It is the paradox of an ever richer, ever more modern superpower, open to global trade, willing to generate mass tourism to four continents; and yet increasingly closed to the circulation of information and ideas. There are ways to bypass censorship, search for news on foreign sites. Vpn networks (Virtual Private Networks) can be used, which bypass the Chinese access routes to the Internet. But you have to have a particular motivation. Moreover, everyone does it at their own peril and risk. Among foreign diplomats, I collect a wealth of anecdotes about "technical incidents" that can affect VPN users. I myself was a victim of it. While traveling in the retinue of an American president, therefore assisted and protected by a team of telecommunications experts who had come from the United States to create an "extraterritorial bubble" around us, I had a day marred by malware that ate my files on my computer. The revenge of the Chinese police? Certainly the use of VPN is monitored. In this too, they are one step ahead of us.

facial recognition technologies : artificial intelligence applied to biometrics, at the service of security. Crime prevention, anti-terrorism: China is a kind of multiple Israel, on a continental scale, in terms of the number of video cameras and 24-hour surveillance. An entire population, the Islamic Uyghurs, have been the guinea pig for a gigantic digital surveillance experiment: passports seized, Internet sealed, biometric and genetic mapping on millions of people in the vast Turkmen province of Xinjiang. Here is Big Brother in action as no Western country can even dream of it; far more advanced even compared to other authoritarian regimes or democrats such as Russia, Iran, Turkey. China is at the forefront and is proud of it: officially this is how it would have defeated the infiltrations of al-Qaeda and Isis among the Uyghurs, the jihadist plots. But Big Brother extends far beyond Muslim Xinjiang. In addition to Tibet, there is also Inner Mongolia, the last entry among the regions to which the foreign journalist or diplomat has no access, except for obtaining special visas. A third of China's territory is off-limits to many of us.

Censorship that advances relentlessly, flanked by increasingly sophisticated forms of biomapping and control over us humans, entrusted to Artificial Intelligence: this China is a *Blade Runner* with blue skies, a dystopian and despotic future, but without the acid rains of the cult movie by Ridley Scott. On my return to China, very strong and contradictory impressions assail me. From Beijing I go to Tianjin, the port city closest to the capital, with 16 million inhabitants and a curious Italian past (we received it as a reward for participating in the Boxer War, we commanded you, also leaving an architectural footprint, since 1902 at the end of World War II). Fifteen years have passed since my first visit and I return to admire a futuristic cultural center, with a marvelous public library with a spatial design, created by Dutch architects. Between Beijing and Tianjin a *bullet train whizzes by every hour*, one of those high-speed trains that now reach all the big Chinese cities. When I left California in 2004 to move to China, there were discussions about building the first high-speed rail line in America, which would connect San Francisco to Los Angeles. It is still debated today. In infrastructure, the United States is sinking, falling apart; China sparkles with modernity (at the end of September 2019 the new Beijing mega-airport came into operation; the last one was inaugurated in 2008 on the occasion of the Olympics).

We got distracted for a moment and some of us still think that the Chinese "copy us". The theft of know-how, industrial espionage, the looting of Western technologies remain a reality; but it does not exhaust the explanation of what happened. A piece of this economy has overtaken America, which has suddenly realized it and tries to run for cover when perhaps it is too late. A turning point was the economic crisis of 2008-2009: both because it absorbed all the attention and energies of the West, making us less attentive to what was happening far from us; and because that crisis gave Xi Jinping the certainty that the authoritarian system is more efficient than liberal democracy in governing the economy and society.

But if we Westerners got distracted and underestimated the Chinese leap forward, it's not just our fault. This China does not allow itself to be easily observed, explored and narrated. The list of American colleagues who have been denied entry visas grows longer and includes some of China's top experts such as Nicholas Kristof of the New York Times, and my mentor, the former rector of the Berkeley journalism faculty, Orville Schell. His case is particularly absurd: he was one of the greatest American journalists expert on China, on which he wrote books that still remain obligatory points of reference; he is married to a Chinese woman; heads the Chinese section at the Asia Society think tank in New York. Denying him a visa is a revenge, a punishment, which deprives him of the possibility of updating himself on the ground. Like him, many sinologists are hit regularly: either they write things pleasing to Beijing, or the regime denies them access to the country which is the object of their studies. It is understood that our knowledge of China must overcome significant obstacles, erected to let us know only what they want. In the days of my last visit, a further element of tension and concern concerns the arrested Canadian diplomats. It is undoubtedly a revenge linked to the Huawei case. In December 2018, the financial director of the Chinese telecommunications giant, Meng Wanzhou, who is also the daughter of that company's founder, former People's Liberation Army officer Ren Zhengfei, ended up under house arrest in Canada. She was arrested at the request of the Justice Department in Washington, accused of violating sanctions against Iran. The story is intertwined with the embargo against Huawei that the United States is also trying to impose on its European allies, due to the suspicion that Chinese technology in 5G (fifth generation) telephony is a Trojan horse of espionage. The clash is USA-China, but Xi has decided to rage against Canadians, trampling diplomatic immunity with arrests.

When I left China, the principle of collegial leadership at the top of the state was still in effect. The then president, Hu Jintao, was a gray figure. The advent of Xi has changed everything: this president is a star, he manages his image like a Western leader, even the First Lady is a celebrity. He has vanquished most of his domestic opponents, often hitting them with corruption charges and heavy sentences. He had the constitution changed to inscribe his name (an honor reserved for the founder of the regime, Mao Zedong). He had all limits on his mandate repealed. Not since the days of Deng Xiaoping - the director of capitalist reforms but also of the Tiananmen Square massacre - has a Chinese leader concentrated such power in his own hands. Xi builds his legitimacy around a hypernationalist narrative: China asserts itself as a superpower with no qualms about exhibiting a hegemonic project; erases forever the "century of humiliations" opened by the Opium War (1839). All this pleased the Chinese very much especially in the initial stage of its ascent.

True cradle of sovereignty, even on a political level, China has preceded us in many experiments. For example, religion rediscovered and valued as a pillar in the reconstruction of a strong national identity. In Beijing where state atheism was born in Mao's time, today I visit increasingly crowded Buddhist temples, with the official blessing of Xi Jinping (Confucius, the lay prophet, was also enlisted for the same function). From Israel - in addition to the technology of video surveillance and biometric controls - this China has borrowed another idea: it finances "discovery of one's roots" trips to young Chinese in the diaspora, an expensive but far-sighted gift, to ensure that the vast community of 'overseas (by now 70 million between emigrants and temporary expatriates) participates in the same nationalist revival of the motherland.

I have a close vantage point on the fate of ethnic minorities; and alternative. My three adopted sons, Shanzha, Che Ghe and Seila, are yi from Sichuan: physically more similar to Tibetans or Mongols; with darker colored skin than the Han (the stock of the Chinese majority). We first met thirteen years ago in their mountain village, Jiudu, Xichang County. When I visited it, there were no sewers, the roads were unpaved, many houses had no electricity or running water. The three boys are now in their twenties and their lives have taken a turn in the big cities. They have remained attached to their roots, they love to return to their native village for traditional festivals in ethnic costume. They proudly display photos of their visits. The Chinese government has invested in the modernization of those remote and poor areas. The streets are paved, their semi-abandoned cottages have received public restoration work. As orphans and members of an ethnic minority, Shanzha, Che Ghe and Seila are entitled to a monthly allowance, a basic income.

The paths to consensus in an authoritarian regime are manifold: they include the construction of a welfare system; the security; the fight against corruption with exemplary sentences; the export of overcapacities (labour, steel and cement) along the New Silk Roads. In terms of national populism, Xi's comes from afar; his muscles are pumped up on steroids. The Yi are a tiny ethnic group, never the protagonist of mass rebellions like the Tibetans and the Uyghurs. But even with those other more riotous minorities, Beijing has always alternated between carrot and stick. The Dalai Lama himself recognized the benefits of the material progress with which the Chinese lifted his Tibet out of medieval misery.

This China reminds in many ways the America of the conquest of the Far West, it has the same spirit of a great historical mission to fulfill. Will those who oppose the relentless march of fate be overwhelmed? Unlike the United States of the nineteenth century, the People's Republic experiences its rise as a return to the natural order of things. Three thousand years of history give it an obvious superiority complex. The supremacy of the white man on the planet is a brief recent parenthesis, which is closing. If the West tries to resist the inevitable, is it only out of selfishness, arrogance, arrogance?

Meanwhile, America is experiencing another "Sputnik moment": this is how the shock of October 4, 1957 was defined when the Soviet Union managed to put the first satellite (called Sputnik, in fact) into orbit. The overtaking of the United States in the space race was then completely unexpected, the event shook the Americans, who considered themselves superior; it forced them to run for cover by accelerating and enhancing their space programs. Today in some technologies such as fifth generation mobile telephony and Artificial Intelligence China has its own Sputniks. Once again, as sixty-two years ago, America must awaken from its torpor and discover that it is in danger of being overtaken. But the challenge with the USSR took place entirely on strategic-military terrain, from atomic bombs to missiles (space was a place for exercises and simulations for vectors that could also be used for war purposes). With China, the challenge is 360 degrees. The Chinese economy is now equal in size to the American one, while the Soviet one has always remained smaller, and underdeveloped in certain sectors. Europe is tugged, disputed and perhaps one day it will be crushed: unlike in the past, in fact, its economy, not limited by the walls and iron curtains of the first cold war, is very integrated with that of China.

Along with nationalist pride, I also sense a sense of unease among my Chinese friends: some fear that Xi is contributing to the very "Thucydides trap" he says he wants to avoid.

Beijing and New York, September 30, 2019

I

The new cold war has already begun

The best of the best is not winning a hundred battles out of a hundred, but subduing the enemy without a fight.

SUN TZU, *The Art of War*, 6th century BC

The origins of the expression "cold war" are disputed among several authors, but the original paternity probably belongs to the British novelist George Orwell, the same one who revealed the communist dystopia in the ferocious satire Animal Farm and prophesied a pre-digital Big Brother in the *novel* by political fiction *1984*.

In 1945, shortly after the nuclear bombings of Hiroshima and Nagasaki, Orwell wrote an essay called *You and the Atomic Bomb*. In that text (published in «Tribune») he foresees the advent of «a peace that is not peace». 1945 is the year of the Yalta Conference, the summit in which the American president Franklin D. Roosevelt, the British premier Winston Churchill and the Soviet dictator Iosif Stalin begin to divide the world into areas of influence. The break between the United States and the Soviet Union, allies in the fight against fascism, has not yet occurred. We will have to wait for the advance of the Red Army and the seizure of power by the Communists in various European countries. A year after Orwell's intuition, the British premier Churchill, speaking in front of the students of an American university on March 5, 1946, launched his alarm about the advent of an "iron curtain": it is the image with which he depicts the geopolitical, military, ideological separation between Western and Eastern Europe.

Orwell in 1945 not only prophesies the new US-Ussr conflict that would mark the world's destinies for the next forty-four years. In his essay he foresees a third scenario and an additional protagonist: «East Asia, dominated by China». Shortly thereafter, in fact, his prediction came true, China ended up in the Communist camp with the victory of the Red Revolution in 1949. Washington refused to recognize the legitimacy of Mao Zedong's government and would have long diplomatic relations only with Taiwan, where the nationalists who fought the communists with American help have taken refuge. It's not just the cold war, soon a real, very hot war broke out between Chinese and American soldiers on the Korean front from 1950 to 1953.

Today's alliance between China and North Korea is a consequence of that conflict. But then the relationship between Mao and the leaders of the Soviet Union deteriorates, leading to an incurable schism between the two churches of world communism. A period of international isolation for Beijing followed. Interrupted by a twist, in the year 1972: Republican President Richard Nixon's trip to meet Mao. It is the beginning of a new chapter, a story of progressive improvement in Sino-US relations. In order not to spoil the new friendship, America "forgives" the military repression in Tiananmen Square (1989), limiting itself to reacting with fairly modest sanctions (which concern only military supplies). Between 1999 and 2001, the fundamental stage of this process was the final negotiation and then the entry of the People's Republic into the World Trade Organization (WTO): the construction of a globalization based on mutual interest, which dramatically expands the borders of the capitalism, profoundly transforms the mechanisms of the world economy, to the point of configuring a sort of condominium. It is the latter the chapter that is closing before our eyes.

There are many signs of a new ice age, a progressive and irreversible estrangement between the two superpowers is perceived. Even tourist flows are affected. Between 2017 and 2018, the number of Chinese visitors to the United States fell by 10 percent, over 200,000 fewer. The enrollment of Chinese students in American universities is also declining. Greater difficulties in obtaining visas, to which is added the dissuasive effect of a climate of mutual hostility. It doesn't help that spies have sometimes infiltrated the Chinese diaspora in the United States. Trump's tariff sweeps on Chinese imports have garnered media exposure and monopolized our attention, but there's a hidden and equally important detail: those protectionist measures have sparked increasingly weakening resistance from American capitalism. Once the rulers of Beijing knew they could count on a formidable ally in Washington: the lobbies that defend the interests of American multinationals.

When Trump began waving the tariff threat in 2017, there was a principle of resistance. From the Confindustria associations to the editorials of the Wall Street Journal, the voice of American capitalism has made itself heard, and as always it has defended open borders. But that battle has faded. Over time, the American capitalist establishment is resigning itself to the idea that relations with Beijing will never again be like they have been for the last thirty years. Many US companies were already "secretly" indignant at having been victims of industrial espionage, blackmail by the Chinese government, theft of technological secrets; but they did not dare to say it aloud in order not to antagonize the authorities of the Asian superpower and not to attract retaliation. Now many chief executives are becoming more explicit in admitting what had been happening for years: with the noose laws imposed by Beijing (for example the obligation to take on a local partner), Western multinationals have "bred up" those competitors who later have gobbled up market share. Until a few years ago, the game was worth the candle, because the looting of know-how had access to a billion consumers as a counterpart.

Gradually, however, that market began to shrink as local produce became more palatable. With some exceptions, the pro-Chinese lobby in Washington is in retreat. Plan B has already been launched in the headquarters of various multinationals: how to make ourselves less dependent on China, how to loosen those ties that had been built up over the last thirty years. It is a surgical operation, painful, almost as if it were the separation of Siamese twins. Just look at an Apple iPhone, symbol of a global logistics chain: the incorporated software and the pieces that make it up come from California, the Chinese province of Guangdong, Japan, Taiwan, Germany. An intercontinental plot that seemed inextricable, but which is now becoming an element of vulnerability. Apple, or any other multinational, cannot afford to be at the mercy of the political storms between Washington and Beijing. The two richest economies on the planet had become almost one; now the divorce is in progress. It will involve a 'global realignment'. World trade will never be the same again.

If one day we look for the starting date of this new cold war, we could fix it on October 4, 2018. The protagonist is not as illustrious as Winston Churchill, but statesmen of that stature are not abundant in our times. It's up to Trump's deputy, Mike Pence, to deliver the speech that we will perhaps remember as the equivalent of Churchill's "Iron Curtain". The place is an important think tank in Washington, the Hudson Institute. It was there that a new American doctrine on China was born in October 2018. Someone ironically called it "the bamboo curtain". But there is little to joke about. The American vice president's speech did not come about by chance; is the concentrate of analyzes anticipated months earlier in the document on the National Security Strategy. China is defined as a «revisionist power», in the sense that the Americans give to this term: a power that wants to «revise», in order to bend the rules of the game, the world balance, the structures and the balance of forces in its favour.

This conclusion is accompanied by a lengthy indictment. China, accuses Pence, has for many years systematically violated the spirit and the letter of the rules on trade established by the World Trade Organization (WTO): it was the first to impose super-duties often much higher than those launched by Trump; forced Western companies to transfer their technological knowledge; stole intellectual property; he used public subsidies without hesitation; it devalued its currency to make made in China more competitive; it has littered the world with spies who steal secrets from the West. These are all fairly well-known things, but in Pence's speech they gain critical mass, they become dominant: not only has the tone changed, but there is an awareness of having reached a point of no return. Continuing to tolerate those behaviors of the Chinese is not possible, except accepting the suicide of the American empire.

A second order of accusations in Pence's speech concerns the betrayed promises by the leaders of Beijing: the opening of the borders that was in the pacts has not come true; China's economy remains a hybrid state capitalism with strong Communist Party control; zero political reforms, indeed since the advent of Xi there has been a marked involution of authoritarianism. The third chapter in the indictment of Trump's deputy concerns foreign policy and military strategy: Beijing continues the escalation of armaments, has launched a militarization of neighboring waters, in the East and South China Sea it is multiplying acts of arrogance to annex disputed islands from Japan, Philippines, Vietnam.

The new cold war – with its official declaration – began with that speech at the Hudson Institute. Which only touches on the issue of the import-export deficit: one problem among many. We are no longer in a trade war between the United States and China. By now it is clear that the imbalances between sales and purchases were only a *casus belli* , a chapter in a much larger clash. It is as if all of a sudden many alarm signals have been turned on, and America has opened its eyes: there is someone who is about to steal its job; and since the challenger also has a political system incompatible with the historical values of the West, the threat takes on an existential, epochal dimension. The allies are called to rally around the United States, or they will suffer the consequences.

All of this does not depend solely on Trump nor does it begin with his presidency. We must avoid the easy temptation to attribute the sabotage of globalization to his nationalist turbo-populism: this is the convenient version that Xi went to expose at the World Economic Forum in Davos, but it does not hold up. In reality, a review of US-China relations had been in the air for some time. This is confirmed by an authoritative American report whose authors are not at all close to this president. However, they acknowledge that they have seen China right, even if the methods he uses are not effective. The threat coming from Beijing is much more serious than the West has understood: economic and technological, political and military, it is an all-out hegemonic challenge, against which we must run for cover.

This was stated in February 2019 by top American experts on China, many of whom are progressives or moderate anti-Trump Republicans; some have played a leading role under the previous administrations (including Democrats) of Bill Clinton, George W. Bush, Barack Obama. Their conclusions are contained in the Task Force Report presented to the Asia Society of New York, and entitled "Course Correction". The document contains the most complete and up-to-date analysis of the state of relations between the two superpowers. Orville Schell and Susan Shirk, who led the work of this bipartisan group of experts for two years, credit Trump for having intuited things that the economic establishment and the upper echelons of diplomacy have been slow to acknowledge. China and the United States are indeed "on a collision course", and not because of American protectionism, which is only a belated counter-reaction to the Chinese one. The crisis in relations comes from afar, it will be lasting, it will have global repercussions even after Trump, whoever succeeds him in the White House. It is China that systematically applies sovereignty: it discriminates between foreign and national companies, "it tramples on the rules of competition and international laws, it violates the fundamental principles of reciprocity". In the technological field it pursues hegemonic designs and, from the fifth generation of mobile telephony to artificial intelligence, aims at a "new form of mercantilism", with synergies between civilian companies and the armed forces theorized in the "Made in China 2025" plan.

America and Europe have been dangerously distracted for many years. The Chinese acceleration towards a new expansionist ambition and an aggressive approach comes from afar: the great crisis of 2008 convinced the communist leaders of Beijing that their authoritarian model is superior to Western liberal democracies; with the advent of Xi Jinping in 2012, the shift towards "nationalist triumphalism" became even more marked. This has coincided with a heavy authoritarian involution of the Chinese regime, which is not happening only to the detriment of its own citizens or ethnic minorities in Tibet or Xinjiang, but also abroad. China is "exporting authoritarian methods" in the ways it uses its economic power to silence criticism. It dictates repression in Hong Kong, threatens foreign governments, maneuvers the granting of visas or cultural funding, blackmails Western scholars and universities to broaden the scope of its censorship. It carries out increasingly hostile acts towards Taiwan and other US-allied democracies, starting with Japan and South Korea.

The advent of Trump has forced China to deal with a counter-reaction, the effectiveness of which does not convince experts, especially those with democratic sympathies. According to them, Trump's mistakes are above all two: he has not been able to build an alliance of interests to force China to respect the rules; and limited litigation to the commercial sphere avoiding any pressure on human rights. «A great strength of America is the network of friendships: it has 60 allied countries in the world, China has North Korea. It is on this force that we must leverage; do not act alone by breaking the front of your allies» reads the report. There are also doubts about American claims in the commercial field: for China to profoundly change its unscrupulous nationalism, which alters the conditions of competition, "it is necessary to confront the communist leadership with a new system of continuous pressures and controls, a path long-term to correct behaviors that are ingrained.

The think tanks Asia Society, Center on US -China Relations, 21st Century China Center sign the bipartisan report. Among the experts who worked on it is the diplomacy veteran Winston Lord, former ambassador to China, former right-hand man of Henry Kissinger. He was in the front row at the summit of the Nixon-Mao thaw that made history in 1972. Today he is worried about "an America that has canceled human rights and democracy from the agenda of its relations with China". As we can see, moderate Republicans and the American democratic left criticize Trump for mistakes; while they fully share the analysis of the Chinese danger contained in Pence's speech that opens the new cold war.

Does it make sense to use the expression "cold war", taking it out of the context of the years 1946-1989? The differences since then are enormous. If desired, they can be summarized in a single figure: trade between the United States and the Soviet Union in the final part of the thaw (when Mikhail Gorbachev ruled in Moscow, at the end of the 1980s) reached a maximum of 2 billion dollars a year, i.e. few things. The one between America and China is worth the same amount, but per day.

The People's Republic is the number one trading partner for many Western nations. At the time of the two capitalist-communist blocs, reciprocal relations were limited, economic integration almost non-existent; while now China is "among us" to the point of buying English and Italian football teams, Volvo, the entire port of Athens. When has the USSR ever been able to buy control of Western, sometimes strategic companies? Furthermore, citizens of the USSR or East Germany had enormous difficulty obtaining a visa to visit the West; instead today Chinese tourists invade Venice, Florence, Rome, the Cinque Terre, London and Paris en masse. Their government does not deny them free movement abroad. Visiting Moscow, Warsaw, Prague still on the eve of the fall of the Berlin Wall was like ending up in a black and white film from the 1950s, so many were the privations and backwardness of communism. On the contrary, traveling to Beijing, Shanghai and Guangzhou today is a dive into extreme modernity, it's like having a visionary taste of what we will be like in ten years.

In short, except for the shock from Sputnik, the USSR has never been a serious economic and technological rival of the West; China has already surpassed us in many respects. Is it therefore illusory to imagine extending a "cordon sanitaire" around the People's Republic, made up of duties or sanctions or other forms of containment? And what is the alternative: unconditional surrender? Will we die Chinese?

Ignoring threats to our security is either naïve or irresponsible. Here is another difference with respect to the US-USSR cold war: in those days, armaments for the defense of the West were built above all by state companies, located on this side of the iron curtain, protected by anti-espionage devices (occasionally a few spies managed to get in, but they were exceptions). Today Western weaponry, including American weaponry, incorporates digital technologies designed and manufactured primarily in the private sector, and often overseas. It is increasingly probable that our defense systems contain components made in China, which could spy on us, or worse, sabotage us from within in the event of a conflict. It's not science fiction, it's the consequence of a world we built at a time when China seemed harmless to us and perhaps even destined to become democratic like us (this was a widespread theory at the end of the 1990s).

There is a Chinese counter-narrative that we need to be aware of. Xi Jinping effectively exposes it, but it is shared by many of his compatriots, authoritative intellectuals or simple citizens. It's the thesis that America is slipping into paranoia, inventing an enemy that doesn't exist. "We lack the imperialism gene," Xi said in September 2017, on the eve of his first meeting with Trump. It is a theory that is taught in the textbooks of the People's Republic: unlike Westerners, China has never had colonies, has never expressed aggressive imperialism, has not built its power by conquering and plundering other people's territories. Three thousand years of history are thus simplified, for the use and consumption of official propaganda. The story is of course much more complicated and the narrative can easily be reversed. Today's China is actually the result of territorial conquests, given that over a third of its territory belonged to subjugated ethnic groups and foreign civilizations (Tibet,

Xinjiang, Mongolia). In the long history of the Celestial Empire there was no lack of bullying towards neighboring countries, forced into forms of vassalage and subordination. Even in more recent history, from the Maoist revolution onwards, there have been wars: against India and against Vietnam. There is no biological "gene" of imperialism; if it existed, no people and no civilization would be immune from it because good empires are regime tales.

In my Chinese years I became passionate about the history of that country. One character in particular fascinated me - the eunuch-admiral Zheng He, who explored distant oceans more than half a century before European navigators opened the era of great discoveries for us. Told by Chinese history textbooks, today Zheng He appears as a benevolent hero, at the helm of a fleet that scoured entire continents without ambitions of conquest or exploitation, driven only by curiosity and the desire to broaden knowledge, exchanges with other peoples . But in recent years that mythical vision has been revised and corrected by more serious historiography: in reality, Zheng He's fleet intimidated the countries he visited to make them compliant vassals. It didn't manage to conquer and build empires overseas, just because the Ming dynasty had to withdraw its military strength to its home territory, threatened by nomadic invasions that would lead to its downfall.

Starting from the distorted reconstruction of his imperial past, Xi's message aims to arrive at a current conclusion. According to him, globalization as it has worked in the last thirty years is a *win-win proposition* , that is, a game that benefits everyone, in which there are only winners and no losers. The rise of China is an inescapable phenomenon as it is the most populous nation on earth. Trump's America is slipping right into the classic "Thucydides trap", as it is recalled and updated by the scholar Graham Allison looking at the Peloponnesian war (5th century BC). According to the Greek historian Thucydides, it was the rise of Athens and the fear it inspired in Sparta that made war inevitable. Allison has studied 16 cases of the last five hundred years in which "the rise of a great nation has threatened the position of the dominant power": 12 of these ended in a war.

Xi takes the "Thucydides trap" seriously to the point that he has mentioned it several times in his speeches, warning us Westerners not to fall into that mistake. According to him, the lesson to be drawn would be that the declining power (in this case America-Sparta) must resign themselves to making room for the rising power (China-Athens) because there is room for everyone in the world and the progress of a new nation does not mean the regression of the others. All the more so if this new power has peaceful goals – to develop economically – and is not threatening anyone. It would therefore be a serious mistake, according to Xi, if America mobilized to stop China. It would fall into a trap that has already resulted in needless tragedies in the past. For example, when Britain became convinced that the Kaiser's Second Reich posed a fatal threat to its security, or even its survival, it shattered a tight network of Anglo-German economic ties and plunged into World War I.

Many Chinese – not just their president – view these Cold War dress rehearsals as a show of arrogance on the part of Uncle Sam. Just as their great country is back to occupying its rightful place in the world - and which was its until the "century of humiliations", that is, until the Opium War of 1839 -, America tries to sabotage its rise because it does not resign itself to losing its supremacy. Arrogance, selfishness, short-sightedness risk dragging the whole world into a spiral of reprisals, at the end of which there is the impoverishment of all. And maybe even a real war. In this version of the "Thucydides trap" there is an evil power, America-Sparta, ready to do anything to arrest its rival; and there is a good power, China-Athens, which has only legitimate aspirations for a better future for its people. In Allison's version, indeed, the Peloponnese metaphor is handled in a much more refined and complex way. The story of rivalries between declining powers and emerging powers is not that simple, there are no good guys on one side and bad guys on the other. Often chains of errors and misunderstandings are triggered on both sides which make the conflict inevitable. Allison does not practice historical determinism, he is convinced that the decisions of leaders can make a difference and prevent rivalries from degenerating into wars. But it does not place all the blame on one side or the other; nor does it accept Xi's Manichaeism about "genetically peaceful" China.

Besides Sparta-Athens and England-Germany there is another interesting historical comparison. It is that with the rise of the United States itself. In the 1800s, Britain was the wealthiest and most advanced nation on the planet;

at the height of his imperial expansion, on his possessions "the sun never set", his fleets ranged over all the oceans. The United States was a typical emerging nation, and it practiced some pirating behavior very similar to that of China today: for example, the patents and copyrights of British companies were shamelessly copied on the opposite side of the Atlantic. (It even happened in the literary field, as the English novelist Charles Dickens discovered in 1842 when he visited an America where his books were printed in large circulation pirated editions without paying him royalties.) American industry climbed to the world's top by imitating and pillaging the inventions of others, from England to Germany. Then, when it was already a strong economy, America knew how to "use" the British Empire to its advantage. It enjoyed the freedom of navigation that was afforded by Her British Majesty's fleet, a beneficial protection for a rising trading power like the United States. So the Americans saved a long time on their own defense costs because London was in the role of «policeman of the world» who enforced the rules of free trade.

Then came the First World War, the conflict that would mark the disintegration or the beginning of the dissolution for many European empires. Even in that war the behavior of the United States - which long delayed its military participation - was opportunistic. They took advantage of the rupture of relations with Germany to expropriate all the intellectual property of German chemical companies on American soil, thus favoring a leap forward in their technologies. They used the model of state capitalism for the construction of modern armaments: the RCA company (Radio Corporation of America) joined the US Navy in the creation of a global telecommunications network. A precedent that the American historian Katherine Epstein, in her analysis published by the «Wall Street Journal» (*To Understand China, Look at America's History*), compared to the close relationship between Huawei and the Chinese armed forces.

Finally, the United States took advantage of the 1914-18 war to support the boom of New York as an alternative financial center to London. They were in many ways a parasitic power, exploiting all the benefits of the Pax Britannica, preparing to replace those who built it and bore the costs. The more educated

Chinese, who know these chapters of our history, wonder why they are accused of behavior that was typical of America in its ascendant phase.

The issue deserves to be explored, because China has effectively behaved like a giant parasite of the Pax Americana. Geopolitical scholars prefer to use another term, *free rider* , which in English designates anyone traveling on public transport without paying for the ticket. Public transport in this case are "public goods available to all", offered precisely by the Pax Americana and largely paid for by the American taxpayer. When China – especially since 1979 – came out of its isolation not only political-diplomatic but also economic, abandoned the principles of communism and under the leadership of Deng Xiaoping began its transition towards capitalism, it found itself it set up vast markets on which to sell its products to drive an industrial boom and lift its citizens out of misery. Those international markets did not exist "in nature", they were the result of an institutional framework which guaranteed their proper functioning. The Pax Americana had been built piece by piece starting with the Bretton Woods summit in 1944. Its pillars were the International Monetary Fund and the World Bank, then those trade liberalization agreements of the GATT (General Agreement on Tariffs and Trade) which decades later they would give birth to the WTO. Even the United Nations was originally an American construction (by Franklin D. Roosevelt). Naturally, the United States had not acted in this way "out of charity" and generosity of heart. Theirs was a postmodern imperial vision, a hegemonic thought also based on *soft power* : the ability to design a world order based on rules, in which other countries could recognize themselves and find advantages.

During the first cold war, the Pax Americana had offered its benefits to "half of the planet", the one that recognized itself in the system of alliances and in the values proclaimed by Washington. After the fall of the Berlin Wall and the disintegration of the USSR, the borders of the Pax Americana widened. Even in military alliances some advantages were offered to a *free rider* like China. Even today, if Chinese tankers can obtain supplies of crude oil in the Persian Gulf and cross the Strait of Malacca unscathed before reaching the ports of Guangzhou, Shanghai and Tianjin, it is because the American military fleets guarantee security against militias and pirates, and ensure navigability of the oceans. The bill is paid by American taxpayers, but the "public service" of the gendarme is also useful to the Chinese.

Someone has defined the postmodern US empire with suggestive neologisms: for example, "empire by invitation" (because it co-opts allies and subordinates rather than making them colonies), "consensual hegemony", "liberal leviathan". The most colossal co-option, and full of consequences, was precisely that of China in the WTO, at the end of 2001. It was perhaps the last act in the enlargement of the boundaries of influence of the American century. The timing must be remembered because even then there were embryonic signs of a potential crisis. China's accession to the WTO, which would have opened up the markets of the whole world, had been negotiated since 1999. But the final act took place in December 2001, that is three months after the terrorist attack on the Twin Towers. George W. Bush was in the White House and his presidency was inaugurated by a serious diplomatic crisis with Beijing. On April 1, 2001, a US spy plane collided with a Chinese military jet in the skies over Hainan Island. A Chinese pilot had died, the American aircraft had been forced into a forced landing, the 24 crew members captured and detained by the People's Liberation Army. The crisis had accelerated awareness in Washington of the formidable Chinese rearmament and interdiction capacity that Beijing's armed forces were gaining in that part of the world. A general rethinking of US-China relations was maturing, fifteen years ahead of Trump. Moreover, even on commercial relations there already existed a critical current towards competition from China and the relocation of American jobs. But then came 9/11, which shifted all of America's attention and energy elsewhere. The People's Republic was then admitted to the WTO at the end of the year, in a world scenario dominated by the "war on terrorism", the military intervention in Afghanistan (promptly supported by China).

Over the years Beijing has developed an ambivalent attitude towards Pax Americana and its various articulations. The Chinese leaders - after a furious internal debate in which the radical wing of the Communist Party feared a "postcolonial" scenario as a result of the opening of the borders - settled within the WTO having negotiated special treatments and favorable clauses. They long accepted the US military presence from the Middle East to the Far East as an element of security and stability for commercial traffic. And they also agreed to fit into the whole architecture of multilateral institutions born out of Bretton Woods, the IMF and the World Bank. At the same time, however, the Chinese leadership has always had a "revisionist" attitude, in the sense of wanting to correct and transform a system that it had already found in force, inheriting it from the American century. It has never ceased to assert, in theory and in practice, its hegemonic aspirations over neighboring seas and disputed territories, including Taiwan. More recently, it has begun building the pillars of an alternative system: the Asian Infrastructure Investment Bank (to which I will return in the chapter on the Silk Roads) is an alternative to the Washington-based World Bank. Nor should we believe that aversion to multilateralism is a prerogative of Trump: the Chinese rulers have never accepted that supranational institutions poke their noses into their abuses against human rights. In short, Beijing practices globalism *à la carte* : it chooses from the menu of the Pax Americana what is needed to advance Chinese power, discarding all the rest.

Seen from Washington, this "parasitic" attitude has become even more unbearable as China now has an economy as large if not larger than America's. Furthermore, the relative decline of the United States is accompanied by very serious internal problems: decades of impoverishment of the less well-off classes, increasing inequalities, crumbling of infrastructures, decay of public schools. Some of these things are related to Chinese competition, some are not. All, however, contribute to making swathes of American voters impatient with their role as "world policeman" in support of Pax Americana. So China's attitude as a *free rider* is opposed by many.

Finally, the long-term strategic-military objective behind Chinese rearmament is increasingly evident. Xi Jinping wants to gradually expel the United States from Asia-Pacific, transforming that area of the world into China's "backyard" where the rulers of Beijing will dictate the law. At times in the tones used by the Chinese leaders there is a return to that conception of the Celestial Empire as the center of a vast system of relations, surrounded by feudal states, vassals and satellites. A sphere of influence in which everyone knows which place belongs to him, and which gestures of obedience and respect are welcome in

Beijing (for example: never invite the Dalai Lama). It is the age-old alternative to Pax Americana's "invited and co-opted empire." It is not a reassuring scenario, especially for those allied countries of the United States that do not wish to become vassals of China: Japan, South Korea, Indonesia, Australia and New Zealand; and India itself which in perspective would be incorporated into an area of the Indo-Pacific under Chinese hegemony. For the Americans, the most disturbing aspect is this: assuming that China is willing to "leave" them Europe and Latin America as spheres of influence at least for some time, the most dynamic part of the world economy is precisely the Asia-Pacific. Adding China, Japan, Korea and India, plus the new dragons of Southeast Asia, we arrive at 50 percent of world GDP. And this is the half of the planet with strong growth: both for the higher development rates and for the capacity for technological innovation.

Relinquishing hegemonic influence over the Asia-Pacific to China means leaving it control over the future and retiring to guard a world in decline. The trap in this case would have been set by Xi Jinping, reserving the best part for himself. To Beijing, all this seems obvious: the aspirations for a dominant role in that part of the world would be the modern version of the Monroe Doctrine, proclaimed by the United States in the 19th century, when they decided to forbid any interference by the old European colonial empires in Latin America. From Mexico down, no one was to hinder the influence of the United States in their "backyard". The fact is that Chinese influence would extend to the most populous area of the planet, and where democracies abound (not negligible detail) whose citizens have freely chosen to side with the West.

I keep a personal memory of China showing its sovereign muscles. The Western media are so "introverted", so obsessed with their own sovereign demons (Trump or Salvini, Orbán or Boris Johnson) that they have not understood how much sovereignty is antecedent and born elsewhere. An original laboratory is China. My memory goes back to the last months of Barack Obama's presidency, when I followed him to the G20 meeting in Hangzhou, the ancient Chinese silk capital which was visited by Marco Polo. Summits are increasingly useless, their ability to decide is steadily declining. However, they are useful points of observation on the relationships between leaders, on the *body language* , or body language, with which they choose to confront their peers. On that occasion, the Chinese presidency that organized the event orchestrated a spite to the American guest. When Air Force One with Obama on board landed on the runway, there were, as always, cameras from all the world's networks to film the leader as he appears at the door of the Jumbo 747 and descends the ladder. It's a scene seen a hundred times, but retains its solemnity. This time, however, the door did not open.

I was in the press room organized by the American delegation in a hotel in Hangzhou for us journalists accredited to the White House. I and my US media colleagues stared at the CNN screen in amazement. Minutes passed. Many minutes. And the door remained closed. The official explanation began to leak from US diplomats: the commander of Air Force One could not open the door for the simple reason that the airport ground staff did not provide him with a ladder high enough to reach the "second floor" of the Jumbo. Time continued to pass, on the ground we saw the US ambassador in China framed by the cameras, and some Chinese notables (but not Xi Jinping). Embarrassment and discomfort were skyrocketing for an unprecedented technical-logistical accident. Finally a ladder was seen moving on the runway, but too low. They put it in front of the "service" exit, a smaller door located low down, under the tail, practically on the "butt" of the Jumbo. Much more time was spent in feverish negotiations between the Americans and the Chinese, but the landlords who controlled the land logistics won. Obama had, for the first time in the history of his official trips, to sneak out the back of Air Force One, in a darkened area under the wings and engines, almost hidden from the television cameras that had waited a long time for him at the exit of 'honor. His arrival was rendered invisible and irrelevant in the set design.

The disagreement was soon forgotten; the American delegation pretended not to notice, avoided raising a case. But woe to underestimate these signals. Chinese diplomacy, which is proud of three thousand years of history, is notoriously attentive to rituals, liturgies and protocol details. There is no worse disaster in Chinese culture than "losing face." Xi had wanted to humiliate Obama that day. Shortly thereafter, Trump won the election, who never misses an opportunity to accuse his predecessor of "naivety and pliancy" in relations with the Chinese. And maybe he's not entirely wrong about that.

Comparing the growing US-China chill to the First Cold War requires examining another key difference. In addition to the economic context, is there an ideological conflict in addition? The Soviet Union waged a war of ideas against the West, paralleled by geopolitical tension and the arms race. Communism was an alternative, hostile doctrine that was offered to the whole world to save it from the evils of capitalism: exploitation of workers, poverty, inequalities, social injustices. In the ascendant era of the USSR, its revolutionary Word penetrated many Western societies, and even more so in the Third World. Marxist ideas were widespread among the workers and the youth; sometimes they were accompanied by the veneration of the alleged "socialist paradise" of Moscow or the Maoist variant. In Italy and France - on "this side" of the Iron Curtain - there were strong communist parties, long in solidarity with Moscow and obedient to its directives. American youth, taking sides against the Vietnam War in the 1960s, were sensitive to the messages coming from the communist world. In developing countries, the Soviet model made inroads in Cuba and in many revolutionary movements that spread throughout the southern hemisphere, from Angola to Indonesia (with mixed success). Indira Gandhi's India adopted an economic socialism inspired by Soviet theories. In short, before imploding due to the failure of its development model, the USSR was a Church antagonistic to the West in every sense.

But China? It is difficult today to find a similarity with the USSR, or with Mao's China which was busy spreading the revolutionary maxims of the *Little Red Book urbi et orbi* . Since the People's Republic converted to capitalism, it has ceased to be a factory of subversive ideologies that aim to undermine Western values. This makes the new cold war very different. More difficult to understand, and to fight. There is no enemy in front of America that declares itself such, like the Soviet Union when it wanted to export communism to every corner of the earth. This has helped to make China "reassuring". After all, the competition between us and them is largely on the business front. It is not an existential question, an irreducible antagonism. This makes it much more difficult to unite the nations of the West and, within them, to mobilize all the energies and all the institutions to unite: as America managed to do after the "Sputnik moment" shock.

Is the absence of an ideological and value competition destined to be only a transitory phase? It is the theme that I will examine in the chapter on alternative political systems and that I only want to outline here. China in the emerging period, in the run-up to the American model, i.e. the period from the capitalist reforms of Deng Xiaoping (1979) to the 2008 Olympics, embraced a sort of political relativism or multiculturalism. He scornfully rejected any Western sermon on human rights. He denounced the (mild) American pressure for democratization as "interference". But he did so without criticizing our political system. Beijing's message was: to each his own. Liberal democracy was born and flourished in the West, so it is suitable for those countries that are its historical cradle, said the new generation of communist leaders from Deng onwards.

China is different for many reasons: size, internal inequalities, Confucian tradition. "Chinese version socialism" became less and less socialist over the years and more and more a blend of authoritarianism, Confucian paternalism, technocracy, and meritocracy. But he didn't pretend to lecture us on how to run things in our home. This changed, first imperceptibly during the 2008-2009 crisis, from which China saved itself (the only major economy to dodge recession) by maneuvering the levers of its dirigisme; then with the coming to power of Xi Jinping, a leader who is convinced of the superiority of his political system. Even the language has changed. Today's China not only does not accept lessons: it gives them. He has no shame in saying that his political structure is more efficient than ours. This is not yet a prelude to an ideological war like the East-West one that raged from the 1940s to 1989. There are no "Chinese" parties, fifth pillars of Beijing's influence at work in Western democracies. However, the new self-esteem proclaimed by Xi, the superiority complex that radiates towards the rest of the world, is already attracting followers in other emerging countries. And it coincides with a phase in which trust in democracy is at its lowest throughout the West.

A footnote concerns the ethnic-racial dimension that can add to the climate of a new cold war. In the United States there are those who have already sounded the alarm about an alleged "witch hunt" launched in universities against scientists, researchers, scholarship holders and students of Chinese origin. In reality there has been a – modest – crackdown on the granting of visas, out of fear that some of these visitors are the Trojan horse of Chinese espionage activity, both in the theft of industrial secrets and in the military field. It does not help that the Beijing government has used the Confucius Institutes scattered abroad to control its expatriate students and researchers.

Talking about witch hunts is exaggerated or at least premature. Just as absurd, disproportionate, the comparisons with the abuses that were perpetrated during the Second World War by the Roosevelt administration against Japanese-Americans: deported to detention camps because they were suspected of being a fifth column of Emperor Hirohito. Nothing like this is happening now, thankfully. For those tragedies of the past to repeat themselves, many principles of American liberal democracy would have to fall, many counter-powers, such as the judiciary, which ensure compliance with the Constitution. Precisely those counter-powers that do not exist in China. There, a witch hunt is always the order of the day: against dissidents, or simply to keep away critically thinking foreign visitors. This does not rule out the possibility that a racial element may intrude into the atmosphere of geopolitical tension in the future. The US-USSR cold war was a conflict between "white Indo-European peoples" and within two ideological systems born in the West: liberalism and Marxism (also Christianity crossed the Iron Curtain, see the Polish Church). Ethno-cultural diversity also separates us from the Confucian Han. It is not the first time that an Asiatic-Confucian civilization has been able to defeat a Western power: the original shock occurred in 1905, when Japan defeated the Tsarist Russia, "white" empire, an event that baffled the entire West.

Another season in which we rediscovered the yellow peril syndrome was the 1980s. The protagonist was still Japan, which invaded our markets of steel, cars, electronics; and bought pieces of American capitalism, from Hollywood to Rockefeller Center in Manhattan. Then an apocalyptic publication was successful which denounced the Japanese invasion, sometimes using racist tones. Then Japan was scaled back with a mix of protectionist measures by

Ronald Reagan. (There was one key difference with present-day China, aside from size: Tokyo is conditioned by a military alliance with the United States on which its security depends.)

American society today is very different from what it was in the 1980s. Ethnic stereotypes, when they survive, have been updated: just look at a Hollywood film – for example *Crazy Rich Asian* from 2018, directed by the Chinese-American Jon Chu – to verify the amazing revenge of the Chinese character. From the times of Bruce Lee and kung fu to those of billionaires or computer geniuses, the road traveled is remarkable. In everyday life in America it is easy to come across positive stereotypes for the benefit of the Chinese: at school it is assumed that they should be at the top of their class in mathematics. In university competitions they buy up scholarships. We are light years away from the Chinese Exclusion Act, the infamous 1882 law that closed the borders to Asian immigrants (after having imported tens of thousands in 1848 to build the transcontinental railroad from San Francisco to New York). Today, if anything, we are almost at the opposite risk: on the other side of the Pacific there is a Han nation with a mono-ethnic culture, with a strong superiority complex not only towards its own minorities but also towards "whites". There is also some analogy with American history here. In the ascendant period of its trajectory, the United States embraced theories such as the "Manifest Destiny", which attributed a divine mandate, a civilizing mission, a predestination to the role of conquerors of the Far West. The theme of the "heavenly mandate" is a constant in the Confucian vision of Chinese emperors.

I return to the «Thucydides trap», and to the research project that Allison led at Harvard University, to extract the rare cases of benign rivalries, those that have resolved without war. I'm the exception, not the rule. A couple of these cases are of particular interest to me. The closest to us, already mentioned, is the handover from the British Empire to the postmodern US imperial hegemony. It wasn't exactly painless because there were clashes: for example in 1956, when the US president Dwight Eisenhower threatened to sink the pound to punish London for the military attack against Egypt at Suez. However, the two nations never fought each other in the phase of imperial transition, indeed, in some respects the transition from the Pax Britannica to the Pax Americana was agreed. The United Kingdom at the end of the Second World War was bankrupt; transferring military bases to the Americans was inevitable, almost a relief, comparable to the sentiment of an impoverished nobleman who finds a wealthy bourgeois willing to buy his ruined castles and pay off his debts. However, this happy exception to the Sparta-Athens model took place in a more unique than rare context: two powers linked by strong kinship ties, blood relations, one a former colony of the other, with the same language, a common system of liberal-democratic values , a culture of the same classics, with American universities originally copied on the British model; and the strong sense of British gratitude towards the power that had stopped Hitler.

Another interesting historical precedent is older, the competition between the Spanish and Portuguese empires at the end of the 15th century. For much of the fifteenth century the Portuguese had been at the forefront of naval exploration and colonial conquest. After the reunification of the kingdoms of Castile and Aragon with the marriage of Isabella and Ferdinand in 1469, and after the reconquest of Andalusia from the Islamic invaders, the new Spain strengthened its overseas expansion and clashed with the Portuguese empire. That rivalry could end very badly, in a classic *remake* of Sparta-Athens. Instead it came to a division of the world into areas of influence, with the decisive mediation of the papacy of Rome. Also in this case, as in the Anglo-American example, the happy conclusion of the Lusitanian-Iberian rivalry was propitiated by belonging to the same Christian civilization.

Values matter, even in the cutthroat world of geopolitics. Today we are facing a challenging superpower that is not only nationalist in the European sense of this term, but defines itself as a state-civilization even before being a nation-state. China, after having undergone devastating processes of homologation to the West (in the economy, in lifestyle, in sexual customs, in urban planning), is rebuilding the complex legacy of its past piece by piece. Its civilization had been, for thousands of years, as distant and as different as possible from the West.

II

Does meritocracy beat democracy?

When I was a correspondent in Beijing from 2004 to 2009, I was impressed by the composition of Chinese governments. Among the ministers, multi-graduates abounded, especially in engineering, other scientific subjects or economics and commerce. There were also ministers who had been top corporate managers, including a former executive at the German Audi group. Many of them had studied abroad. The percentage of Ph.D.s (PhDs) was higher than any Western government. The level of expertise was not casual, but the result of a deliberate and systematic selection.

But Chinese meritocracy is not based only on academic qualifications: as we know, it is not certain that an excellent professor is also good at governing, nor that a manager in the private sector is effective as a minister. Therefore, in addition to academic qualifications and professional experience, the selection of rulers in Beijing looks at their results: they have usually been tested in the lower rungs of power, as mayors of cities (many Chinese urban centers have the population of medium-sized nations European: more than 20 million each Beijing and Shanghai; over 30 million Chongqing) or governors of provinces (Guangdong has more inhabitants than Germany). They arrive at national summits after demonstrating what they can do in local administrations.

Another facet of Chinese meritocracy struck me as they observed their ability to reverse the brain drain. From the outset, the People's Republic had a similar problem to Italy: especially at the beginning of its economic boom, when the gap with American salaries was still enormous, the elite of its talents was attracted to the large universities of the United States, where , once they graduated, they had incentives to stay, given the opportunities offered by California's Silicon Valley, by the research centers of large universities, by multinationals.

They were also attracted to America by the entrepreneurial culture, the ease of setting up their own business, of transforming an invention into a business: just as happens to Italian "brains" on the run, young and old. But unlike Italy, China later managed to bring many back. The return streams of Chinese talent are substantial. Beijing succeeded where Italy failed. First of all, it has made "golden bridges" from an economic point of view, offering those who returned ever more competitive salaries and also abundant funds for research. But not only. The thing that struck me most – it was already evident in my years of Chinese life – was Beijing's ability to offer the talents of the diaspora not only money but also power. Expatriates who had succeeded in American academia were offered leadership positions leading entire university departments and research centers. This is the exact opposite of what usually happens in Italy, where certain university barons envy those who have been successful abroad and work to sabotage their return, or keep the "brains" repatriated on the margins of the system, without granting them managerial roles .

The Chinese case is astonishing, because even in the scientific field it contradicts one of our prejudices. We think a priori that an authoritarian political system should distrust those trained in the West; that he prefers to keep in leadership positions only those who have always been submissive and obedient to the palaces of politics, under the watchful eye of the bosses. Surprise: the Chinese meritocracy is much more flexible and courageous in co-opting those trained by broadening their horizons abroad to the top.

These are signs that perhaps force us to review our stereotypes. Are we sure we have clear ideas about exactly what the Chinese system of government is? Or about the state of the competition between that authoritarian regime and our democracies? Are we certain that the future belongs to political systems based on party pluralism and elections by universal suffrage? And if so, are we in principle, why do our values dictate to us, or because democracy convinces us with its results? Many questions. The answers are getting more and more complex. Perhaps until the great economic crisis of 2008 we were more certain about our political superiority and the universal validity of our values. Today the balance sheet of the challenge is more ambiguous, given the concrete results of the Chinese model and given the crisis of confidence afflicting the West.

For seventy years, from 1949 to today, the Beijing regime has never stopped calling itself communist. These seventy years, however, are not marked by continuity. They must be divided into several periods. Certainly, a clear break is represented by the death of Mao (1976), because shortly after his successor Deng Xiaoping scuttles the ferociously egalitarian communism, renounces radical experiments such as the Cultural Revolution of the Red Guards, inaugurates economic reforms, leads the transition towards the market economy. From 1979 onwards there was a gradual opening up, not only to private property and foreign investment, but also to the possibility of travelling, to the circulation of Western fashions and consumption, to new lifestyles, to the sexual revolution and to many other changes in customs.

Another turning point in the country's political history is the tragic 1989, the democratic revolt, the military repression, the Tiananmen Square massacre. The lesson that the ruling group, from which Deng purged the democratic reformists, draws is twofold. On the one hand there is the clear refusal to follow Mikhail Gorbachev in the political liberalization that will lead to the end of the USSR; on the other there is a drive to accelerate economic modernization even further. To avoid further revolts after Tiananmen, repression is not enough, we need to give more well-being and more material freedoms. A corollary is the co-optation into the Communist Party of the new elite: young graduates, urban upper middle classes, professionals, entrepreneurs, a social base from which to extract an efficient technocracy. Also rediscovering that imperial tradition that had aroused the admiration of... Voltaire: a public administration selected on the basis of strict exams and competitions (before the French Revolution, public offices in the Ancien Régime were hereditary or sold to the highest bidder).

The last date that we should perhaps add as another turning point is 2012, because it marks the coming to power of Xi Jinping. He is a new type of leader, a forerunner of our sovereignty and also of our populism. Xi systematically foments the nationalism of his fellow citizens; furthermore, a basis of consensus was created by launching the campaign against corruption. While he puts senior party leaders in prison, or even sentenced to death, for stealing, Xi concentrates exceptional powers upon himself and cancels the time limits on his mandate from the Constitution.

This China has abandoned many principles of communism. It has publicly traded companies that rival American giants in capitalization, and billionaires that figure in the world's top ten; inequalities are now comparable to those of other capitalist nations. An important exception remains, a continuity never denied since Mao's time: the absolute power of the Communist Party.

Its value system has been evidently evolving for years, with the recovery of the Confucian tradition. But Kung Fu Ze or Master Kung (Confucius is the Latinized name), who lived from 551 to 479 BC, left behind a complex teaching which has been reinterpreted several times. The multiple seasons and variants of Confucianism have accompanied the evolution of the various imperial dynasties. Even the Japanese, Korean and Vietnamese civilizations were marked by the thought of Confucius. The version that appeals to Chinese leaders today is the latest paternalistic-authoritarian interpretation given by Lee Kuan Yew, the founder of the modern city-state of Singapore, in the 20th century. Among the aspects of the Confucian legacy on which the Singapore model is based is meritocracy: by linking up with the ancient tradition of the exams with which one accessed the upper echelons of the mandarinate, i.e. the bureaucracy of the Celestial Empire, Lee Kuan Yew wanted to entrust the city to a ruling class selected not by the voters but on the basis of competence. The results have been spectacular. Singapore, which in the late 1950s was a black hole of Third World misery, is today an opulent technopolis, one of the most modern, efficient and wealthy cities on the planet.

China cannot compare to that micro-model, having 1.4 billion inhabitants. But even its ruling class, by adapting some recipes from Singapore, has achieved phenomenal results: in a quarter of a century it has lifted 750 million people out of poverty, an improvement in well-being that has no precedents in the history of humanity. And he did so with a regime that we are still struggling to define. Terms such as "communist", but also "dictatorial", are inadequate: they are good for North Korea, not for the Chinese government, which allows its citizens to travel abroad freely, to study in American universities, to choose work they want, to get rich. It certainly is authoritarian, given that its leaders are not elected by the people and wield the tools of state censorship or police repression with determination. However, there is also a limit to authoritarianism, since it is clear that the regime wants to ensure mass consensus, which does not come from an electoral mandate, but from performance, from the results of government action.

Chinese politicians are judged implicitly by their peers on the basis of the benefits they offer to the population: work, income, security, education, health. As for authoritarianism, it too is explicitly justified by drawing on the Confucian vision. Simplifying the Master's thought, the sovereign is like a good family man whose responsibilities are extended to the entire nation and who therefore must take care of the well-being of all the members of his community. The latter, however, have duties of obedience; they must put harmony, the collective interest and stability before individual rights. There is a sovereign ethic, very demanding in terms of honesty and self-sacrifice, dedication to the general interest; and there is an ethics of the governed, who have so many duties before having rights. Confucian-paternalistic-authoritarian-meritocratic is perhaps the long definition that best describes this regime. And it forces us to question some of our certainties.

The West is experiencing a profound identity crisis, a fall in self-esteem. The liberal democracies have lost the trust of large sections of the population; perhaps only in the 1920s and 1930s were there such strong anti-democratic currents among us. A key moment in this loss of confidence was the great crisis of 2008-2009, a dramatic accelerator of degenerative processes that had already been underway for decades: the frightening increase in inequalities, the impoverishment of the working classes, the financialisation of the economy, the arrogance and greed of the money oligarchies, the immorality of too many politicians. All this took place while at the helm of the liberal democracies there were "traditional" ruling classes: regularly elected by the citizens, sometimes even selected on the basis of technocratic skills.

In fact, we cannot forget the role played by the "experts", economists and central bankers in the lead, unable to spot and prevent the 2008 crisis, co-responsible for creating its causes. Or of those technocrats who imposed the inflexible parameters of the stability pact on the Eurozone, inflicting on it a decade of stagnation. Some communities of citizen-voters reacted to the shock of 2008-2009 by bringing to power the opposite of the technocrats: thus we have the new populist ruling classes (Donald Trump, Boris Johnson, the 5 Star Movement) who openly declare their contempt for traditional experts. But in terms of the results of government action, things don't look any better. And so the distrust in the ability of democracy to select good governments remains or is accentuated.

One observation is necessary. Even in America and in those European countries where liberal democratic traditions are older, many citizens adhere to them not so much out of deep convictions of values, but only to the extent that those political systems are able to deliver results. The period of greatest consensus towards democracy coincided with the "glorious thirty years" following the Second World War: when the reconstruction boom generated employment and growing well-being, allowed for the financing of welfare, mass schooling and the improvement of medical care , in a context of solidarity and redistribution that kept inequalities within acceptable limits.

We are staunch democrats until democracy fails us. From the moment it ceased to be synonymous with full employment, rising expectations, order and security and well-being, large gaps have opened up in popular consensus. That's normal. We don't fall in love with a political system just because it corresponds to an abstract ideal described in our Constitution or in the books of Montesquieu and Tocqueville. If that system produces inept and dishonest ruling classes, we are assailed by doubts about its validity.

It is in this context that in 2015 the book by a Canadian scholar who theorizes the validity of the Chinese system arrives like a bombshell. The volume, now available in Italian (*The China model. Political meritocracy and the limits of democracy* , Luiss University Press, 2019), is an uncomfortable essay, which has aroused controversy, especially in the United States where someone has accused it of apology for the authoritarian regime by Xi. The author is Daniel A. Bell, professor in China at Shandong University. His work starts from an in-depth knowledge of Chinese history and Confucian thought, which is rare among Westerners. It is an invitation to humility, for anyone convinced of the superiority of our political systems. Bell writes:

The practice of choosing a country's top leaders through free and fair competitive elections has a relatively short history (less than a century in almost all countries, compared to – for example

– the 1,300 years of the imperial examination system in China). Like any other political system, it has advantages and disadvantages, and it seems too soon to claim that it is the best system of all time. More fundamentally, it seems peculiar to take an almost dogmatic position in favor of a system that does not require experience and expertise from its leaders. There are many ways to wield power – in the workplace, in schools, hospitals, prisons, and so on – and in those settings the natural assumption is that experience is needed before leaders wield power. No company or university would choose a leader without substantial leadership experience of some sort, preferably in the same field. Yet political power is an exception: it is acceptable to choose a leader who has no previous political experience, as long as chosen with the mechanism *one person - one vote.*

Bell does not despise the founding ideas of liberal democracy, he admits that having the equal right to participate in national politics has been considered in the West "a key to human dignity". It recognizes that «voting is a collective ritual that produces and strengthens a sense of civic solidarity; when we vote we feel part of a community». Those who live in America like me are reminded of the great battle of blacks in the 1960s to defeat those Southern states that took revenge on the Civil War by denying the right to vote to the descendants of slaves. The victory of the civil rights movement led by Martin Luther King was rightly experienced as a civilizational achievement. Denying African Americans the vote had been a way of diminishing their humanity.

And yet this unifying value of the right to vote has weakened: in the United States, Europe, India, democracies in recent years are no longer able to create a sense of civic solidarity. On the contrary, the popular vote exalts divisions, up to extreme, lacerating polarizations. Putting a ballot in the ballot box is often no longer seen as a civil rite that makes us sharers in the same nation, but as an act of war against our enemies, who don't think like us. In recent election seasons, the trend is to divide into hostile ideological tribes, which delegitimize each other. Finally there is high abstention, many are called out, they think that voting is useless.

Surely the philosophical halo of the spiritual fathers like Montesquieu and Tocqueville does not serve to "sell" electoral and multi-party democracy to the Chinese. As Bell explains, "Political surveys find that citizens of East Asian societies typically understand democracy in substantive rather than procedural terms: that is, they tend to value democracy for the positive consequences it leads to rather than value the procedures." democratic in itself". In this sense, the performance of China, which saved itself from the recession in 2008-2009, while Europe and America were sinking into a serious crisis, seems a clear verdict: Beijing has been governed better than Washington, London, Berlin or Paris. Bell also takes into consideration other Western scholars critical of democracy, for example the economist Paul Collier (author of *The Last Billion*, Laterza, 2009) who demonstrated how party democracy exported to poor countries with ethnic divisions tends to increase violence. Xi Jinping subliminally conveyed this message to his citizens when he gave great visibility in the state media during the 2016 US election campaign: the coarse brawl between Donald Trump and Hillary Clinton perhaps seemed in itself defamatory to the reputation of democracy American.

Bell's essay was seen by some as an attack on the West, in an already difficult phase: the number of democracies in the world regresses (after the period of expansion between the 1970s and the fall of the Berlin Wall); in America and Europe, voters are showing increasing signs of absenteeism or despising their own governments; in autocratic regimes there are those who theorize our decline, like Vladimir Putin. Bell does not want at all costs to convince us of the superiority of the Chinese model, however he refutes some of our stereotypes with these four statements: «1) for a political community it is good to be governed by high quality leaders; 2) China's one-party governing political system is not about to collapse; 3) the meritocratic aspect of the system is partially good; 4) can be improved». There is food for thought, even if the events in Hong Kong cast doubts on the ability of Chinese technocrats to predict and manage crises when they go beyond the purely economic sphere.

Bell's merit is also to explain in detail how exactly the selection of the ruling classes works in China. For better or for worse. It cannot be said that the People's Republic is a "pure" meritocracy. It is clear that to get to the top you need to be co-opted by those who are already there. The exams to be passed concern first of all party loyalty. There are currents within the CCP, even if they are undeclared; clans, consortia command you. However, these systems, while typical of a single party that has a monopoly of power, have not generated a sclerotic, incapable and bankrupt ruling class like that of the Soviet Union in the years from Brezhnev to Cernenko. As for corruption: it exists, but it is not so pervasive and voracious as to kill development, unlike what happens, for example, in many African or Latin American countries. Chinese leaders who steal do not steal so much that they impede economic modernization and dynamism. Meritocracy therefore works because in order to make a career in the CCP, in addition to the traditional criteria of loyalty to the top, to this or that clan of power, criteria of efficiency and competence apply.

How is this efficiency measured? In a Western democracy we trust the wisdom of the voters to do it: we have the right to kick out a party or a president who has failed us after four or five years; consequently this sanction should serve us to select capable managers. Unfortunately this is not the case. Lately some of the oldest western democracies fail to do this. What criteria did China use? In the past, when a rising leader was sent to be mayor of a large city or governor of a region (the Chinese call them provinces), the metrics were the growth of gross domestic product, incomes, Work. If the leader exhibited good economic results in his area at the end of his mandate, he was most likely promoted to a higher level. A flaw of this criterion is that it uses only a quantitative measure of economic development. Indeed, China has grown impetuously, but has overlooked some problems: the plundering of environmental resources first. Another real risk is that local administrators, to make a good impression on Beijing, will pursue growth at all costs, financing "cathedrals in the desert", useless infrastructures, huge residential complexes that remain uninhabited, all covered by the public debt. This also happened. The Chinese boom has many dark sides, hidden prices, which will come to light over time. However, we must not believe that the managers have been selected and promoted only on the basis of the GDP of their area of competence.

From 1979 to today many things have improved in China, in addition to the material standard of living: the quality of teaching, health, longevity. The condition of women has made progress: the current level of emancipation and women's rights in China is on average higher than that achieved in Indian democracy. All this happened without the instability of democracies; and within a framework of order, with low crime levels. Moreover, in recent years the Chinese leadership has tried to change the criteria for selecting future managers: for example, environmental sustainability and pollution reduction parameters have also been added to evaluate the performance of local administrators. Polls are increasingly being used to gauge the mood of the population, so even if Chinese people don't vote, their opinion of rulers is somehow recorded. At the peripheral level election experiments have even been introduced: not with different competing parties, but with different candidates in the same Communist Party.

The People's Republic is not the only case of modernization successfully managed by an authoritarian political system. In the Far East, in addition to Singapore, South Korea and Taiwan also had their economic "miracles" in an era in which they were dictatorships: right-wing. Today's Vietnam is a "communist" variant that attempts to replicate the Chinese model.

Some traditional objections to the authoritarian model are famous. Among the most important is that of Amartya Sen, Nobel Prize in Economics as well as humanist philosopher of Indian origin and professor at Harvard, in the United States. Sen contrasted the electoral democracy of his native country with communist China. He pointed out that even when India was very poor, it managed to avoid mass famines the size of the one caused by Mao's infamous Great Leap Forward, the policy of forced industrialization which caused a collapse of agricultural crops. Some estimates put the number of Chinese who died between 1958 and 1961 at 30 million as a result of the Maoist Great Leap. Sen notes that in a system where citizens can oust rulers through free elections, mistakes and crimes of that gravity are avoided or corrected more quickly than in a one-party system with absolute powers. They are the antibodies and immune defenses of a democracy. His diagnosis remains true, but it doesn't necessarily apply to China as we know it today: since 1989, not even the CCP has made such serious mistakes. Indeed, in terms of development in the last thirty years China has beaten India; and it is even surpassing it in the fight against pollution, more recently.

There is another thesis with which we Westerners have reassured ourselves of the superiority of our democratic system (I too, because you will find traces of these arguments in my books *The Chinese Century* and *The Chindian Empire*). It's the theory called the "middle-income trap." I summarize it like this. An authoritarian system that has given good results in ferrying an underdeveloped country towards prosperity runs into serious difficulties once it reaches a "middle-income" level. That is, a per capita income located halfway between the old rich countries – such as America, Europe, Japan – and the emerging countries. The initial takeoff is typical of a phase in which the emerging country has a majority of peasants, a low-productivity workforce moving to the city with industrialization, and leaving the fields to work in factories generates a powerful increase in productivity. Then that phase ends; a mature stage of development occurs, in which the rate of growth typically slows down. (Of course, it has already happened in neighboring Asian models: Japan, South Korea.) This slowdown is associated with demographic aging, which is happening at great speed in China today. An aging population in turn causes a decline in economic performance.

Once you reach that halfway mark, so many new problems crop up. Citizens are no longer satisfied with economic growth, they begin to ask for quality of life, therefore new rights and protections. They want guarantees on the air they breathe, the water they drink, the food they consume. They want to be consulted before a nuclear power plant or high-speed rail is built on their doorstep. They want a fair welfare. Furthermore, the more they have studied, the more they become infected by ideas circulating in the media and on the Internet. They wonder why they can't have the same freedoms and rights as others: for example as we Westerners, who have the power to oust the rulers. In short, the same authoritarian regime that had managed the take-off from poverty to industrialization well becomes too rigid to respond to the new questions of the citizens.

To these pro-democracy arguments we can add, icing on the cake, the Silicon Valley theorem. It is the idea that freedom of expression is essential to nourish technological innovation: creative geniuses are rebels, someone like Steve Jobs came from a hippy culture, transgressive and disobedient to the rules. In the long run, an authoritarian system loses the competition with a democratic nation because it does not offer the conditions for an equally dynamic and innovative economy. This whole set of objections has been part of our culture for many years. I remember that when I went to live in California (in 2000) Bill

Clinton and Bill Gates in unison launched the same prophecy: «The Internet will inevitably bring democracy to China». Twenty years have passed and we are still waiting for it. (Meanwhile, maybe the Internet has created some problems for our democracy.)

Around the same time, at the turn of the millennium, from my observatory in San Francisco I began to make regular sightings on the opposite side of the Pacific. I happened to accompany an American delegation during the negotiations for China's accession to the WTO. I clearly remember that even then, in the year 2000, there was a rich American publicity which predicted the imminent end of the Chinese economic miracle, overwhelmed by debts or environmental instability or some other crisis. Even that prophecy has been slow to come true for twenty years. In the meantime, the "Silicon Valley theorem" itself is creaking, because the Chinese do not just copy, they have become capable of innovating independently. The prophecy of their collapse is always in time to prove right, mind you. The calendar of history is full of surprises, crises never happen when we expect them. Authoritarian systems, due to their opacity, sometimes manage to keep the precursory symptoms of a collapse hidden until the very end. However, perhaps we should begin to ask ourselves if perhaps we are not using the wrong criteria.

Given the originality of Daniel Bell's provocation, I spoke directly to him about the «China model». I was inspired by a phrase by Vladimir Putin. In an interview with the "Financial Times" on the eve of the G20 in Osaka (June 2019), the Russian president said that Western liberal democracies are doomed because they do not provide the results that the majority of their citizens want. This criticism would be much more credible if it came from Xi Jinping. The Chinese government has been obtaining - for some time - far superior results to the Russian one.

That's exactly what I asked Daniel Bell. Here are his answers, in the interview we conducted remotely while he traveled between China and Canada in the summer of 2019.

Why is Xi not as aggressive as his Russian counterpart in attacking the prevailing ideas among Western elites?

"Unlike Putin, Xi does not feel a direct political threat from the West and therefore does not seek to undermine the political system of Western nations. Moreover, Xi recognizes that different political systems are suitable for different countries, based on the size of nations, their culture, specific national conditions. Xi's vision is widely shared by Chinese intellectuals and reformists. It does not mean denying that there are universal political values such as the right to life, protection against torture, against genocide, against slavery; or that there are global problems for which global solutions are needed, such as climate change or nuclear weapons. But we should admit the possibility that different countries use different mechanisms to select and promote their rulers. Western nations with a long history of liberal democracy can use elections to choose leaders; China with its long history of political meritocracy can use meritocratic mechanisms to select and promote its leaders. Western democracies should improve in terms of coherence with the liberal democratic values they profess; political meritocracies should improve in their adherence to meritocratic values. These are widespread views in China. So Chinese leaders don't cheer for the fall of liberal democracies until the West interferes in their choices."

In your book "The China Model," you defend meritocratic governance systems, where leaders are selected based on their expertise. In many Western democracies – the United States, the United Kingdom, Italy – absolute or relative majorities of voters have turned their backs on the concept of meritocracy, distrusting the experts and the technocrats. Those who elected Donald Trump, Boris Johnson or Luigi Di Maio do not seem to be looking for professionalism or experience. Is the West moving in the opposite direction to the Chinese model?

«One can speak of a Chinese model only in a Chinese or Asian context. I link it to the ideal of a "vertical democratic meritocracy": where democracy prevails at the lower levels of government, meritocracy prevails at the top, and there may be experiments between the two levels. It is not necessarily relevant outside the Chinese context. Having said that, meritocratic elements also exist in Western liberal democracies and these have indeed been weakened in recent years. In the United States, for example, the electoral college system was meant to provide guarantees against incompetent and immoral leaders, but that guarantee no longer works. In Europe, the European Union was conceived to ensure meritocratic governance at the central level, but those mechanisms no longer work. And with the rise of populism in more recent years, there are even fewer safeguards to prevent "the people" from choosing leaders without experience and a track record of competent policymaking."

Since «The China model» came out in its first edition you have been subjected to criticism in the West. They almost accused her of being a tool of Beijing's propaganda.

«My book is the defense of a political ideal – vertical democratic meritocracy – which I use to critically evaluate the reality of China. I show that there is a large gap between that ideal and the Chinese reality. For some reason many Western critics believed that I was defending China as it is, its status quo. Maybe it's the title's fault, talking about a Chinese model can give that wrong impression. In China, however, my intentions are clearer. And to begin with, the Chinese title is "Political Meritocracy": it refers to the ideal rather than the reality. Incidentally, my Chinese publisher said that in its entire history the censorship had never imposed so many cuts on him as they did on my book. We eventually managed to recoup most of those cuts, for example by replacing a Wall Street Journal quote with an official Chinese source claiming the same thing. In any case, the critical spirit of my book is undoubtedly clear to Chinese readers, who understand that I am defending an ideal model, not their political reality.

She lives and works in China. How much has your book been discussed, including the most critical parts? How open is the political debate among the people after years of "curing Xi Jinping"? How visible is the tightening of censorship in your eyes?

"My book has been widely reviewed and debated. The reaction is almost diametrically opposite to what I have raised in the West. Since I defend an ideal Chinese system in which there is democracy at local government levels, and meritocracy in the highest echelons of central government, the most widespread criticism in the West is that more democracy is needed at the top. On the contrary, the most widespread reaction among Chinese readers is the request for greater meritocracy at the bottom. Because elections in villages are often marked by corruption and citizens do not derive benefits. However, there are also some liberal reformists in China who criticize me because they would like to judge their political system using typically Western canons and do not share my judgments on vertical democratic meritocracy.

The protests in Hong Kong seem to prove her and the supporters of the Chinese model wrong. First of all, because the citizens of Hong Kong, despite being Chinese, do not want that model at all. Secondly, if Beijing's rulers are really so experienced and competent, why were they displaced by the protest? Why haven't they seen the causes mature?

"Political leaders in the real world cannot predict the future, nor prepare for all scenarios. What they can do is learn from their mistakes, and a meritocracy works best if rulers know how to draw lessons from mistakes and accidents. So far, fortunately, Chinese leaders have not used a brutal crackdown - Tiananmen Square 1989 style - on the unrest in Hong Kong. At the time of the previous wave of protests, the so-called "umbrella movement" in favor of democracy, the rulers let the students get tired and disturb the rest of the citizenry, until the protests died down by themselves and peacefully. We have to hope that it will happen again, although the protests this year have become more violent and may require more vigorous measures in the future if the violence continues. If Chinese leaders made a mistake in Hong Kong, it may have been that they granted too much political autonomy under the "one nation, two systems" formula. If Chinese leaders had exerted more pressure for an education that teaches more Chinese history and culture (each country prioritizes its own history and culture in school, thus political identities are generated) and for meritocratic mechanisms that guarantee Hong Kong of the most competent and wise leaders, many problems would have been avoided. But to see an improvement of this type we will probably have to wait for the "one nation, two systems" formula to expire in the year 2047 [the year in which the 50-year Beijing-London agreement signed in 1997 at the time of the return of Hong Kong to the motherland, *NdA*].»

How does a meritocratic political system avoid isolating itself from the criticisms of its citizens when it makes mistakes? How does he ward off the temptation of "eternal power"? How does it not turn into a self-perpetuating oligarchy, preventing citizens from eliminating it if they are unhappy with it?

«I see the disadvantages of the meritocratic system, including the risks of abuse of power and fossilization. I propose ways to avoid those risks, without resorting to competitive election at the top. When I wrote the first edition of my book, the number one problem was the abuse of power for profit, that is, corruption. Since then, strong anti-corruption measures have managed to reduce it significantly. Yet that anti-corruption campaign has affected so many government officials that today there is no shortage of political opponents seeking revenge against the current government. This in turn has made the current leadership more paranoid, and explains such a decision as the lifting of time limits on Xi Jinping's term. So we are all over again, grappling with the risk that the leaders do not want to give up power. Fortunately, there is still a system of collegiate leadership that prevents the establishment of a personal dictatorship in the style of Mao.

It seems that the world is unwittingly advancing towards a new kind of cold war. It all started with a trade conflict, then a technological conflict, and now we are coming to a head-on geo-economic confrontation between the United States and China. What do you think of the "Thucydides trap" scenario, often cited as a cautionary tale by Xi? Does a clash of civilizations, a conflict of values, also have to do with making that scenario ineluctable?

«The big problem is this America which seems determined not to give space to a rising power like China. But no power can remain "number one" economically, politically and culturally forever. China can do more to reassure that it poses no threat to the United States. It must reinforce and reiterate the message that its political system is fit for China and not for export. It can also do more to show that it wants to cooperate with the United States for the common good, to provide "global public goods": why not offer, for example, joint naval patrols in the Asia-Pacific region? But in the end, things will only calm down when the American people choose a leader who can realistically manage expectations and appeal to the better sides of human nature.

These theses of Bell deserve attention. I retain a good deal of skepticism. I have seen the grimmer, arrogant and overbearing side of the Beijing regime up close. In other books such as *Mao's Shadow* I recounted my misadventures with the Chinese police while reporting in Tibet and Xinjiang where ethnic riots had broken out. Here I want to recall instead the mishap that befell the largest American newspaper. It is a punishment that comes between the end of 2012 and the beginning of 2013, and "punishes" the "New York Times" for having dared to investigate the private wealth of Chinese leaders. On several occasions, for four months the important newspaper was the victim of incursions by cyber-pirates, attributable to the Beijing government.

Chinese hackers have systematically attacked the New York Times, breaking into its computer systems, stealing the passwords of its journalists and other employees. The timing of the cyberattacks coincides with the publication of several investigations, which began on October 25, 2012, on the wealth accumulated by the family members of the Chinese premier at the time, Wen Jiabao. A patrimony of over 2 billion dollars, built practically from nothing: Wen Jiabao is a government official who could not have such huge means, but has placed family and friends at the top of state-owned companies and semi-public financial institutions. Exploiting those positions, the prime minister's family members have carried out operations that closely resemble inside trading, "shrewd" investments thanks to confidential information.

Computer security experts to whom the "New York Times" asked for assistance have collected evidence on the methods used by Chinese hackers, similar to those used by the Beijing army. (The Chinese military has repeatedly orchestrated similar attacks against sites of the Pentagon, the State Department and other US government agencies.) During the raids, the e-mail account of Shanghai correspondent David Barboza, who had signed the investigation into the Wen family's assets. To conceal the origin of the attacks, the Chinese hackers "passed through" the sites of some American universities, following a method already used in the past to hide their tracks. In addition to Barboza, 53 other New York Times employees had their passwords stolen and their emails hacked.

The story started badly and ended worse: with the shutdown of the New York Times website, today inaccessible in its Chinese version to anyone who does not use the (dangerous) anti-censorship systems known as VPNs. The political timing of this story is interesting. Wen Jiabao had arrived on the eve of retirement. He was part of the CCP current defeated by the rising star, Xi. The latter may have been – according to some versions – the hidden director of the revelations about the Wen family fortune. First he used the American newspaper to hasten a rival's disgrace. Then he "blinded" the "New York Times". Also because in the meantime the hunt for news on the rich communists had made converts. The Reuters agency had begun to deal with Xi's family. She's obscured too. The leaders of this China are undoubtedly capable, but they have an allergy to transparency that seems to denote insecurity.

Finally another little personal memory from my trip to Beijing in July 2019. There is no better place to observe the Chinese enigma than a wonderful newly opened public library. A work of art, and a disturbing metaphor for the Chinese model. One of our adopted daughters, Shanzha, joined us from Sichuan and was able to stay with us for four days. Shanzha is 23 years old, she is making great progress in English, we enjoy the long conversations. My wife organized a trip from Beijing to Tianjin with her. A large port city with 16 million inhabitants, I visited Tianjin when I was a correspondent in China to discover a particular attraction: the Italian quarter, perfectly recognizable for its Art Deco style of the early twentieth century. Relic of that period from the turn of the century to the end of WWII when we commanded that city.

This time our destination in Tianjin was a brand new public work, of which my wife Stefania had read marvellously: the Municipal Library, a jewel of avant-garde design, the work of the Dutch studio Mvrdv. Binhai Library is the nucleus of a multipurpose cultural center, which includes concert halls and public recreational spaces. They designed it with refined elegance: in the center a maxisphere dominates an immense entrance hall, around the sphere the various upper floors of the library can be glimpsed like thin membranes. Or some clouds. Or circles drawn in the water when a stone falls into it. After admiring the overall aesthetic, however, one begins to observe the details. And you are amazed. From afar it looks like a cathedral whose walls are made of books. Layers of shelves packed. A postmodern version of the legendary Library of Alexandria. When you get close to the walls though, you find that most of the books are just drawings. Beautiful view from afar, disappointment up close. The expedient has a practical reason: the floors are so high that it would be absurd to put books there, they would remain inaccessible.

But the trompe-l'œil trick is a kind of allusion. The library is full of real books. But when I explore the sections in English, I realize that only technical, scientific, IT, managerial and business works abound. Almost nothing concerning history, political science, sociology. Nothing that would inform a Chinese reader of what we think about China. The wonderful library is a mirror of what Xi Jinping has imposed on their Internet. Tool of modernization, but also of isolation and closure.

Although the prophecies of catastrophe have so far always been denied, I maintain my skepticism about the authoritarian system. Maybe because I'm conditioned by my western culture. Or perhaps because I have seen other "models" rise, shine, seduce the world, finally set. It may be that the China model escapes the rule. It may instead be like all the others: valid for a season, not for eternity.

III

The war for technological supremacy

———

Is it true that Beijing has already overtaken us in the race for artificial intelligence, fifth generation telephony, the "Internet of things", i.e. the new digital revolution that will transform the economy and society? Is China also close to the primacy in supercomputers and "quantum technology"? With what consequences? Has the time come to rigorously filter the Chinese companies authorized to invest in our home, or even the Chinese students admitted to Western universities, due to the danger of espionage? And what damage could a retaliation by Xi Jinping inflict on us, for example in the strategic sector of "rare earths"? There are many questions gathering on the horizon, on difficult terrain for non-experts. Precisely because these are complicated issues, and the interests at stake are immense, we also have a legitimate suspicion of being manipulated, by one side or the other.

In the US-China challenge one thing is now clear: the real stakes are no longer just the import-export imbalances, macroscopic but all in all adjustable. The new cold war will have to decide a winner in the race for technological supremacy. It is a challenge in which technologies for civilian and military uses mix and mingle, the boundaries between business and security, or espionage, are increasingly ambiguous. It is a war that will more and more often impose painful (and costly) side choices on Europeans, faced with ultimatums: even regardless of Donald Trump's bullying, there will be less and less room for ambiguity or "third ways" , it will be necessary to take sides either with Washington or with Beijing. The big difference compared to the First Cold War is in fact this: the USSR was a war and also an ideological superpower (when the communist Gospel was at the peak of its worldwide diffusion), but it always remained an economic dwarf, little integrated and little influential in the international exchanges. China has an economy equivalent to the American one, and has already deeply penetrated the industrial and financial fabric of all Western countries, as well as in Asia, Africa and Latin America.

This configures an unprecedented scenario. Chinese technology is already among us, from smartphones to the antennas that control their traffic, while we were never penetrated by Soviet technologies during the Cold War. Not even in the most improbable political fiction thrillers could one imagine an America addicted to computers manufactured in the Soviet Union in the 1980s. Today, Huawei smartphone sales are a multiple of Apple iPhones. Regardless of the label and the brands we buy, we are unable to say how many parts of an intelligent product to which we entrust all sorts of secrets every day (even trivially our bank accounts) are made in China. Freeing ourselves from this addiction, if it is necessary and if it is still possible, will not be easy or painless.

Even in the so-called "trade" negotiations between Washington and Beijing, the most significant data is the list of issues that are on the table, as presented by the White House. In the first place is "intellectual property", that is, everything related to the protection of know-how, industrial secrets, on which America accuses China of systematic thefts. In second place is the theme of "technology transfer": this includes the disputed Chinese regulations which oblige many Western multinationals to hire a local partner by revealing all technological secrets to him; and also the sale to China of those American technological products (semiconductors, microchips and electronic memories) that have ended up under embargo.

Ten years after my return to the United States, the balance of power between the two superpowers has changed enormously compared to the period 2004-2009 when I lived in Beijing. At that time it was clear who was number one and who was number two, who was the teacher and who the pupil. While I have returned to China regularly, about once every year, I didn't immediately feel the speed of catching up or overtaking in key areas of advanced technologies. But I'm not the only one. The whole of America, and in particular Silicon Valley, was distracted at the wheel and did not see the approaching fireball in the rear-view mirror. It was a Ferrari with Chinese plates in the fast lane. Now America is trying to run for cover, but it could be too late. From Washington policy makers to the top executives of West Coast digital giants, everyone has committed the sin of *complacency* : a mixture of complacency and conceit, a belief in one's own superiority.

One of the first to sound the alarm was, not surprisingly, a Chinese-American (US citizen of Chinese origin) who has a life divided between the two shores of the Pacific Ocean. Kai-Fu Lee is originally from Taiwan - as such he is not suspected of political sympathies towards the communist regime in Beijing - and grew up in the United States, where he did his studies. Then his management career took him to China as the head of the local Google branch. Finally he set up on his own, does venture capital, has an office in Beijing and finances Chinese start-ups in the artificial intelligence sector (which the Americans designate with the initials AI, from Artificial Intelligence). In 2018, he dedicated a book to this sector: *AI Superpowers: China, Silicon Valley, and the New World Order* . The essay is an authoritative call to America to wake up from its slumber. Kai-Fu Lee uses the comparison with "the Sputnik moment": that is, the shock that hit the Americans in 1957 when the Soviet Union preceded them in the first step towards the conquest of space, putting the Sputnik satellite into orbit. Even in that case, the scientific competition between the superpowers had obvious military implications, because those who had an advantage in rocket technology could also use it to transport nuclear warheads instead of satellites. The Sputnik shock was a healthy jolt: John F. Kennedy, after winning the presidential elections in 1960, launched the race to the moon and many other research programs with public funding. Even on the military ground, America never really let itself be overtaken, or not for long periods.

A Sputnik-shock, according to Kai-Fu Lee, was suffered first of all by China: when an artificial intelligence made in the USA, the DeepMind AlphaGo software by Google, managed to defeat one of the world's leading experts of the oldest «strategic game » Chinese, that Go that connoisseurs consider much more complex than our chess. The event, which went almost unnoticed in the West, seems to have convinced the Chinese leadership of the strategic importance of artificial intelligence.

Today it is America that must suffer another Sputnik-shock. Kai-Fu Lee warns that in future technology the Chinese are overtaking the West. And not just by dint of copying. Certainly the systematic looting of intellectual property has allowed the beginning to catch up, but Kai-Fu Lee underlines the importance of other phenomena. Piracy has also damaged many Chinese companies, victims of unscrupulous local competition. China is truly a Wild West of intellectual property, where know-how, patents, discoveries are poorly protected and often copied with impunity. However, at least if one looks at the prosecution statistics, 95 percent of trade secret thefts would come from Chinese companies themselves. This piracy has also had positive effects: it has generated an ultra-competitive environment, stimulating an entrepreneurial culture that is just as widespread as the American one and even more combative. In the end, if many American digital giants have had to withdraw from the Chinese market, it is due to a mix of factors: from pure and simple protectionism to the underestimation of local talent. In the case of social media like Facebook and Twitter there has been censorship; but for Amazon it can be said that the defeat came from local competitors who are better at understanding the needs of Chinese consumers. It is striking to observe that back in 2012 the then president of Google Eric Schmidt declared: «The Chinese will not be able to build a modern society based on knowledge as long as they practice censorship»; but today the number of Chinese users of the Net has exceeded the sum of those of the United States and the European Union; Google as a search engine has only 1.7 percent of the Chinese market, while its local rival Baidu has 75 percent. There are at least three other factors that weigh in the race for AI supremacy and it is necessary to analyze them carefully.

First. The saying that in the age of AI "data is the new oil and China is the new OPEC" (the name of the oil cartel led by Saudi Arabia) is fashionable. This is connected to Deep Learning: machines capable of learning by themselves are the new generation of artificial intelligence, the one that replaces us humans in many fields of activity. To excel, Deep Learning - «deep learning» - needs to digest an immense mass of data: Big Data. A country with 1.4 billion inhabitants has an evidently larger data collection basin.

Second. The authoritarian nature of the regime can be an advantage as it ignores restrictions on data collection. We Westerners try – albeit with limited success – to protect our privacy. The Chinese are used to and resigned to being spied on by their government. In many cases, the Chinese Big Brother tramples human rights with impunity: see the biometric and genetic mapping of millions of Uyghurs, the Muslims of Xinjiang. But all of this helps fuel AI in key areas like facial and voice recognition. In America, it is mainly young people who surrender to the reality that Amazon, Facebook, Instagram and Google collect all sorts of information about them; in China since Mao everyone takes it for granted that the state knows everything about their private life. To follow: the "social credit" experiment with which Beijing accumulates information on each citizen and then assigns him a sort of civic report card with multiple uses, including in the economic and financial fields. There is an evident synergy, made up of alliance and complicity, between the police Big Brother and the innovative capacity based on the extraction of data from each individual.

Third. The Chinese political system is a mixture of capitalism and communism, with a strong dirigiste imprint. In Kennedy's time, America too was a dirigiste and in fact public funding for science and research was decisive for the conquest of space. Today's America is very different, it passed through the neoliberal revolution of Ronald Reagan, then also embraced by democratic leaders such as Bill Clinton and Barack Obama. Administrations of all political stripes have become convinced that Silicon Valley is self-sufficient and single-handedly guarantees America's leadership in advanced technologies. Their *laissez-faire* contrasts with the robust intervention of the Beijing government. The People's Republic actually intends to catch up and surpass the United States in many leading sectors. The approach used for overtaking is diametrically opposed to the American one: it is a "top-down" strategy, that is entrusted to the top-down planning of the government authorities, which must lead to the flowering of market initiatives. The same difference exists in the world of research, where the Chinese one is «mission driven» (guided by a mission), the American one retains a «curiosity driven» component (free research, not oriented towards a fixed objective).

The American model has proved superior in the past, but that doesn't mean it will always be. President Xi theorizes that the state must support the "national champions" of digital: the three Bats (for "bats" in English), acronym of Baidu-Alibaba-Tencent; plus some niche excellences such as iFlytek, specialized in *voice intelligence* or speech recognition. Beijing now accounts for 60 percent of all global investment in AI One Chinese municipality, such as the city of

Tianjin, allocates more government subsidies to AI companies than the federal administration in Washington does for the entire United States . The city of Beijing has spent $2 billion on a technology park reserved for start-ups in the sector. Armed with this massive state aid, China has already surpassed the United States, the European Union and Japan in the number of scientific researches and patents in AI

All this brings us back to what is at stake in the negotiations between the two governments. A twist occurred when Xi Jinping suddenly reneged on his promise to reform China's intellectual property laws in spring 2019. The about-face displaced Trump, who believed he already had victory in his pocket. It was following that change of mind that the American president launched new duties, to the point of affecting almost all products made in China. In a sense, Xi has thrown off the mask: he ended up confirming American fears that for China what matters most is not to invade the world with products, but to dominate it through technological supremacy. Trump reacted by embargoing Huawei, the Chinese telecom giant that is at the forefront of fifth-generation mobile telephony, the gateway to the "Internet of Things". Xi Jinping, in turn, has threatened to deprive American industry of "rare earths", essential for many technological products. These are the first moves of the new cold war, perhaps the worst is yet to come.

World War II truly became a planetary conflict when Japan attacked the United States at Pearl Harbor on December 7, 1941, giving President Franklin Delano Roosevelt the final push for direct military intervention. In the Japanese narrative that treacherous attack, without a formal declaration of war, had become inevitable because America was putting the economy of the Rising Sun in difficulty with an embargo: not so much of raw materials (although Tokyo was dependent on oil American) but of machinery, airplanes, technologically sophisticated products. Almost eighty years later, we are wondering about similar scenarios, after the embargo decreed by Trump on the sales of semiconductors made in the USA to China and Xi's threat to take revenge by depriving the West of precious minerals which are indispensable for our electric batteries, computers and smartphones. In the field of advanced technologies, the United States and China seem to be about to fall into the

"Thucydides trap", the inexorable showdown between a hegemonic power in decline and a power on the rise that aspires to leadership.

The semiconductor embargo intertwines and in part coincides with the Huawei case. This colossus, born from an offshoot of the People's Liberation Army, has been accused by Washington of every wickedness: theft of American and European industrial secrets, strategic espionage in the service of Beijing, and even violation of sanctions against Iran (for this The last charge in December 2018 was arrested in Canada with a request for extradition to the United States the financial director of Huawei, Meng Wanzhou). Trump's embargo to block sales of American components to this company went into effect in May 2019 and forced Google, Qualcomm, Broadcom and other companies to freeze their supplies to Huawei. In the case of Google, for example, it was decided to stop selling certain Android software that is installed on Huawei smartphones. Qualcomm, on the other hand, is one of the major suppliers of microchips, intelligent memories that are the soul and brain of mobile phones. The embargo has also affected the sales of other US companies such as Microsoft and Dell and extends to non-US companies, such as South Korea's Samsung and Japan's Panasonic. It is enough for these multinationals to incorporate 25 percent of US-made components in their products for them to automatically be subject to the Trump administration's measure.

Silicon Valley and its surroundings have protested this embargo which also harms America. In the past, US companies exported $300 billion worth of semiconductors to China annually. These same companies are subject to counter-retaliation and retaliation from the Beijing government which has drawn up its own list of reprobates, "unreliable" companies banned for obeying Trump's directives. This embargo has opened up a new scenario. All the major players in the global economy need to revise their medium to long-term forecasts. Many of the mechanisms that had made the world more homogeneous, integrated, complementary to the point of symbiosis will be dismantled. None of this stems from Trump's protectionist frenzy. The "trap" is a mechanism that comes from afar, towards which changes that began long before he became president converge.

For a couple of decades, China had been free to build its own Internet behind that new Great Wall of censorship. The People's Republic has caught up and surpassed us in many digital technologies, but mixes little with us. He doesn't use the same social media as Facebook, Instagram and Twitter are banned. He doesn't use the same messaging apps: Weixin replaces WhatsApp (that too is prohibited). The brave few who want to challenge censorship get around it with VPNs – Virtual Private Networks – but they do so at their own risk. The vast majority of Chinese are comfortable in that separate internet, behind the fences built by their government. Thanks to the skill of local entrepreneurs, the Chinese Network makes daily life easier. A single app like Weixin concentrates trades that here belong to WhatsApp plus Facebook plus Amazon plus PayPal plus eBay plus Uber, Airbnb, Booking and many more. With a click on a single app you have all the services of the digital economy at your fingertips on your smartphone display. This is not the kind of Great Wall that surrounds North Korea's gulags. Behind the high fence of protectionism and censorship, China has unleashed the energy and creative imagination of a people who were the first to invent writing, printing, gunpowder and even capitalism.

Late, America responds by building a wall of its own. The embargo - even if it will have exceptions and truces - is Washington's attempt to react to that separation that Beijing has planned long in advance. The American retribution identifies a prevailing strategic threat but also an Achilles heel of Chinese industry. The most immediate strategic threat - the Huawei case - is that China conquers world supremacy in fifth generation telephony, 5G, a technology that could lead us towards a new digital dimension: the "Internet of things" is an expression that evokes new frontiers for robotics, automation, artificial intelligence, for example the ability of objects at our service to talk to each other and exchange information (with civil and even military implications). China's weak point is precisely its dependence on semiconductors made in the USA. As on the eve of Pearl Harbor, the Americans are trying to block the rise of their rival by depriving it of essential resources. But this raises new questions. How was it possible that China reached the 5G milestone first, ahead of America? How effective can the embargo on semiconductors made in the USA be? What are the scenarios that open up now?

The first question, on Chinese overtaking, has no clear answers. I choose the one that seems to me the most documented and convincing, summarized in an analysis by Charles Duan, *Why China is Winning the 5G War*, which appeared in «The National Interest» magazine on February 5, 2019. On the one hand, there is an American pathology that I know it well, having analyzed it years ago in my book *Master network* : the degeneration in the patent war. Silicon Valley, as I wrote five years ago, has become the «Valley of Lawyers»: the Masters of the Net fight each other less and less on the ground of innovation, more and more in the courts. Or, even before reaching the courts, in the accumulation of arsenals of patents which mainly serve to dissuade new competitors: high legal barriers erected around the oligopoly, to protect themselves from outsiders, crystallize the balance of forces. If a new Steve Jobs were to be born today, perhaps he would do what many young founders of start-ups do: as soon as they find a winning idea, they go public and then sell their micro-company to a giant; it would be almost impossible to repeat a miracle like Apple, which is the building of a great enterprise from scratch.

In Duan's analysis in the dock for the delay in 5G there is Qualcomm, the San Diego company (which is not exactly in Silicon Valley but in Southern California) that has been at the forefront of innovation for telecoms, but today it is above all at the forefront "in the most convoluted legal strategies". In short, America has wasted time and has accumulated delays in 5G because the pace of innovation has been slowed by the absence of real competition. At the same time, Chinese investment in 5G has already surpassed US investments by $24 billion. And Beijing plans $500 billion in 5G investment over the next decade. On the one hand we have an American model based on *laissez-faire* , which however is no longer based on true market freedom given that the new monopolists manage to stifle competition. On the other hand, there is a Chinese model that manages to combine a strong public presence, government dirigisme with important resources, and a true entrepreneurial flourishing.

This in part recalls another chapter of past challenges between the United States and Japan. In the 1980s it seemed that the Rising Sun was able to surpass America in many areas, thanks to an original combination of statism, public planning and private capitalism. Then Republican President Reagan managed to stop the Japanese invasion with his protectionism. Trump hopes to do the same with China. Chinese leaders believe they are something very different from 1980s Japan. To begin with, the demographic size of their country is tenfold. Certainly the first lesson they want to draw from the current clash is this: accelerate the march towards self-sufficiency.

Xi's new strategy can also be described with an ancient word: autarky. But applied to very modern sectors. He had to fall back on this defensive mode, after the humiliation suffered by Trump in 2018 on a case that was the forerunner of Huawei. ZTE, an acronym for Zhongxing Telecommunication Equipment, has been in Washington's sights since the time of Barack Obama. It is one of two Chinese telecom hardware giants (the other being Huawei) whose forays into US hi-tech are under fire. ZTE has around 75,000 employees, is a multinational operating in 160 countries, manufactures smartphones and telephony infrastructure. Its smartphones compete in the low-price range and are particularly popular in emerging countries. But, like many products in this sector, they also incorporate technology made in the USA: as has been said, America remains one of the leading producers of microchips, modems, as well as operating systems branded Microsoft and Android (Google). American suspicions about ZTE go back many years. Already during the Obama administration, the White House and Congress blocked some acquisitions by ZTE in America, for the almost certainty that these investments would have been aimed at industrial espionage.

The *casus belli* that brought the American punishment on ZTE was its decision to sell smartphones to North Korea, thus transferring US-made technology to a country under embargo. After the first warnings from Washington (under Obama), ZTE should have taken measures against its managers responsible for the illegal trade to Pyongyang. On the contrary, those executives have been rewarded. The violation is serious, therefore the US Department of Commerce has adopted the measures required by law, prohibiting American companies from having any economic relationship with ZTE. A very hard blow: the company, once deprived of the made in USA components, found itself unable to produce smartphones and other devices. It has therefore rapidly spiraled into a spiral of crisis, with plant closures and the announcement of mass layoffs. A real thud for one of the jewels of Chinese industry, and on which Xi is betting as part of his "Made in China 2025" plan, intended to conquer a leadership in advanced technologies. In May 2018, at Xi's personal intercession, Trump temporarily lifted the embargo. In doing so he prevented ZTE from going bankrupt by immediately laying off tens of thousands of employees. A soothing gesture, but one that certainly hasn't diminished Beijing's alarm. In the future, Xi does not want to find himself again having to beg from the US president for a postponement of the death sentence for a large Chinese technology company.

ZTE's lesson was capitalized on by Huawei's founder and chief executive, Ren Zhengfei. His company wants to forge ahead to become autonomous in the production of semiconductors and microchips. It's a race against time: between an America that hopes to stop the Chinese advance "before it's too late", and the rival power that has no intention of stopping there. For the more pessimistic Western observers, and for Trump's opponents, the American president with his embargo is even accelerating the next leap forward of the Chinese computer industry, i.e. autonomy in semiconductors. For his supporters, however, Trump is opening the eyes of America and some of its allies to a danger that has so far been underestimated. Certainly the Huawei affair raises questions. How is it possible that a company still unknown in the West until the last decade has acquired such a dominance in 5G in a short time that entire European nations are giving it carte blanche to build the future telephone infrastructure? Does anyone still remember when the big telecommunications companies were "ours", that is, Europeans like the Finnish Nokia, the Swedish Ericsson, the German Siemens and the French Alcatel, or Americans like Motorola?

On Huawei, the «Wall Street Journal» recalled one of the first episodes of piracy, which dates back to 2004, when an executive of that company was stopped by security guards at a Chicago technology fair while he was photographing complex equipment from AT&T , Nortel Fujitsu. It was prehistory. In the subsequent stages of its meteoric rise, Huawei continued to use unscrupulous methods, but in a much less artisanal way. The same "Wall Street Journal" in a monumental investigation entitled "Champion or serial thief?" (*China's Tech Champion – Or Serial Thief?* , May 25, 2019) summed up the seven golden rules that the former People's Liberation Army officer imposed on the company he founded. First, don't announce your presence: for many years Huawei has used shadow companies and different names (FutureWei in the US, Atelier in Sweden) to muddy the waters on the ties between its overseas subsidiaries and the parent company. Second, total secrecy and impenetrability: to the point that the offices in Texas and Stockholm have protections similar to military bunkers. Third, gain market share by systematically undercutting your competitors by 20 or 30 percent. Fourth, shameless copying: in a plagiarism lawsuit brought by Cisco, Huawei settled without admitting guilt, but its copies were so identical to the original routers that even computer viruses replicated them. Fifth: even better than copying is having spies inside competing companies, for example a close relative of the founder Ren Zhengfei who worked at Motorola and stole its industrial secrets. Sixth: offer rich rewards to those who, as above, steal secrets from the competition. Seventh: Recruit former competitor employees.

The results have been rewarding. Today, Huawei operates in 170 countries, has 188,000 employees, and in 2018 achieved $107 billion in revenue. And now it apes the multinationals of Silicon Valley also in offering employees sumptuous headquarters, under the banner of quality of life. Perhaps with a touch of kitsch from the nouveau riche Chinese: the new Huawei research campus, in the city of Dongguan, divides its 18,000 scientists between replicas of Italian Renaissance palaces, German Gothic castles, Spanish villas; with Illy espresso machines and French bistros for the lunch break. In fact, after the era of secrecy, Huawei has made a strategic turn by investing in public relations. It organizes press conferences continuously, invites journalists from all over the world to visit its factories and research centres. I know something about it too: suddenly, my inbox was targeted by barrages of press releases from Huawei. In the war of communication it has adopted Western methods.

The image offensive has its reason. Since the beginning of 2019, Trump has put pressure on all allied nations - from Europe to Australia, from Canada to New Zealand - to stop buying complex telecom infrastructure from Huawei. Those devices, according to American intelligence, are the Trojan horses of Beijing's espionage, for both civilian and military purposes. According to Washington, much of the West risks being captured by a vast surveillance network that

Beijing will use at will. We are becoming vulnerable and have only a vague idea of what is at stake. Huawei's answers are unconvincing. Even a traditionally liberal newspaper like "The Economist", very critical of Trump's protectionism, observes that "Huawei cannot persuade its customers with the promise that it will never help the Chinese government and espionage". In Beijing we know what the real hierarchical relationships are between the political power and the capitalist establishment. No Chinese chief executive could say no to a request for "cooperation" with the state and its armed forces.

For reasons of national security and fears of espionage, Washington has blocked the completion of a gigantic US-China telecom infrastructure: the new "fibre-optic highway" under the Pacific, the Light Cable Network for which 11,000 kilometers of cables have already been laid submarines from Los Angeles to Hong Kong. It is another sign of the geo-economic drift of the continents, the new cold war we have actually entered. That titanic project, which crosses the seabed of the largest of the oceans, had important financiers behind it: Alphabet-Google and Facebook were among the promoters of the investment, to improve connectivity and the speed of data flows between the two coasts of the Pacific. The $300 million invested in laying the underwater cables was supposed to ensure the new network was up and running by early 2020. Everything is now stalled for review by Team Telecom, a federal agency in Washington in which the Justice Department, the Pentagon, and Homeland Security (counterterrorism) participate. In the past, other cable networks under the Pacific were approved and are in operation. But today the climate has changed. The large submarine networks, through which most of the global Internet traffic passes, are subject to new supervision. By the way, Huawei equipment is often used in those networks.

Telecommunications and Internet infrastructure are just one of many strategic sectors where America suddenly feels that overtaking China is possible. In supercomputers, whose multiple uses range from medical research to the simulation of nuclear tests for military purposes, at the beginning of the millennium the People's Republic had only two of the 500 most powerful and fastest machines in the world. Ten years later he had already taken first place with the Tianhe-1A, a machine that however still needed Intel microprocessors, designed in California. The Americans promptly banned Intel from selling microchips to China's four largest supercomputer labs. Useless: already in 2017 another Chinese supercomputer (Sunway Taihu Light) again conquered the primacy of the world ranking for power and speed, and this time it was all homemade, including microprocessors. More than a third of China's supercomputers are manufactured in labs directly owned by the military.

To what extent was America itself hastened the beginning of its own end, by underestimating its rival or by naive faith in the virtues of open markets? Doubt has been raised, also with regard to supercomputers, by looking at the role of Chinese scientists who had trained in the great Western universities. The next generation of supercomputers could multiply the brain power of those machines thanks to "quantum technology", the new field of engineering that draws on the discoveries of quantum physics and quantum mechanics. China is investing heavily in this sector, from which it expects applications in different directions: from sensors capable of seeing beyond the smoke or around the corner to other police-military applications. All linked to a prodigious leap in the speed with which information is processed.

Quantum technology exploits the properties of atoms, electrons and photons to open a new chapter in the history of progress: but at the service of which political project and which system of values? Once again, the People's Liberation Army was a driving force in allowing Chinese scientists another symbolic overtaking in 2018: filing twice as many patents on quantum technologies as American scientists. But at the origin there is the figure of a pioneer, Pan Jianwei, a scientist with a professorship in Heidelberg, trained at the Chinese university and then in Vienna, then returned to his homeland to lead the national efforts in quantum technologies. With a goal immediately inspired by security issues: the scholar told the "Washington Post" that he felt motivated when Edward Snowden, the former American intelligence officer, revealed the espionage activities of US intelligence via WikiLeaks (Jeanne Whalen , *At heart of quantum rivalry: economic, security concerns* , in The Washington Post, August 19, 2019).

Pan Jianwei's story resembles that of many other "sea turtles", as the Chinese define the talented expatriates who return home: like turtles who (apparently) feel the irresistible call of their native nest. Now America is trying to be less generous than in the past in training these brains. To begin with, the Washington government has put obstacles in the way of a Chinese program called "Thousand Talents". It's a fund that generously funds foreign experts willing to do research in China, and it's been particularly successful among Chinese-Americans (but not just them). The shutter is also closing on the multi-year collaboration relationships between prestigious American universities - such as the Massachusetts Institute of Technology (MIT) and Rutgers University - and Chinese companies that commissioned advanced research such as iFlytek: an artificial intelligence company closely linked with the Chinese police are possibly compromised in domestic espionage against the Uyghur ethnic minority.

More generally, the climate of incipient cold war is enveloping the 360,000 Chinese students enrolled in American universities. It is one of the paradoxes of the rivalry between the two superpowers, and perhaps it says a lot about the still unresolved inferiority complexes of the Chinese elites: it continues to be a status symbol to send one's children to study in America. It is even for the top leaders of the communist nomenklatura: the last four presidents of the People's Republic have had offspring with US degrees, Xi's daughter studied at Harvard. Under the Trump administration, the granting of student visas to young Chinese has become more stringent. Cases of rejection have become more frequent than they once were. This crackdown should come as no surprise to those in charge in Beijing: the granting of visas to stay in China is notoriously arbitrary, subject to the absolute political discretion of the government, which does not hesitate to ban entry to anyone it deems unwelcome. Instead, American retaliation was vigorously denounced: in July 2019 a World Peace Forum hosted in Beijing's Tsinghua University accused America of racism, of a witch hunt equivalent to McCarthyism in the 1950s, of paranoia about the "Yellow Peril" . In the background there is the suspicion that an envious and vengeful America wants to prevent China by any means from regaining its rightful primacy among nations.

Whether it's out of spite or simple coincidence: on Chinese TV one of the new successful series is entitled "I'm coming to see you overseas", it stages the stories of parents who go to visit their children in American colleges and find them in conditions quite distressing. In one of the episodes, a Chinese father plays the hero because he foils a shooting-massacre, before the arrival of the American police. The fact that various governmental or parastatal organizations of the People's Republic (from consulates to Confucius Institutes) have been discovered to monitor their student population in American colleges, recruiting informants, does not help to calm the climate. In the incipient glaciation there is also this datum which serves to mark the differences from the first cold war: dissidents fled from the USSR who asked for political asylum in America; from China the exodus of dissidents has greatly reduced, after the shock of Tiananmen 1989. Indeed, a research conducted on Chinese students in American universities describes them mostly as politically indifferent, rather nationalists, not at all inclined to bring the climate back to China of freedom and tolerance they enjoyed in the West.

Precious earths or rare minerals: will this be China's secret weapon in the spiral of retaliation and reprisals against the United States? Xi Jinping has on several official occasions alluded to the seventeen rare minerals over which China has a dominant position. They are used in magnets and in many technological devices, from smartphones to tablets. The complete list is here, with the relative symbols: cerium (Ce), dysprosium (Dy), erbium (Er), europium (Eu), gadolinium (Gd), holmium (Ho), lanthanum (La), lutetium (Lu), neodymium (Nd), praseodymium (Pr), promethium (Pm), samarium (Sm), scandium (Sc), terbium (Tb), thulium (Tm), ytterbium (Yb), yttrium (Y). President Xi, visiting a company that extracts, processes and exports rare earths, wanted to send a signal to the United States: we can strangle Silicon Valley by turning off the export taps. In truth, this had happened before, and this time it didn't end well for the Chinese. They tried to use the same blackmail a decade ago, when they imposed quotas on exports. They then had to eliminate them after a conviction by the WTO. Above all, they realized they had scored an own goal.

It is unwise for an exporting power like China to cut its exports to hurt customers. Among other things, the United States imports relatively little of those rare minerals. The main recipients are other Asian countries, from Japan to Singapore. Or Chinese companies located in the complex logistics chain, whose final recipients can also be Apple or Tesla in Silicon Valley, but only at the end of a long journey. Rationing rare earths has the consequence of questioning the reliability of the Chinese supplier, with the result of speeding up the search for substitutes (and China, however dominant, does not have a monopoly on those minerals). However, you never know. In a scenario of progressive inactivation of bilateral relations, nothing can be excluded anymore.

But if the embargo on rare earths remains - as I write - only virtual and threatened, yet another operation has already been underway for years. It is the construction of a Chinese semi-monopoly for lithium. To be precise, lithium carbonate, essential for many technological products, especially electric car batteries. Given the boom in electric cars, the Volkswagen group has predicted that world consumption of that compound will double in just three years. Lithium is not properly part of the rare earths, moreover its production also takes place in Mexico, Chile, Argentina, Australia, Ireland. In all of these countries, however, two Chinese groups – Ganfeng Lithium and Tianqi Lithium – have acquired control or equity stakes in local producers. US companies have been wiped out. 67 percent of lithium battery cells today are made in China, compared to 9 percent in the United States. If the future belongs to electric car technology, the future also risks being Chinese in this sector. Maybe it's already too late to run for cover. Assuming we feel the need to.

IV

The New Silk Roads

———

If you don't know the plans of neighboring lords, you can't make alliances; if you don't know the conformation of mountains and forests, dangerous landscapes and marshes, you can't move armies... Think carefully before moving; the one who first knows the direct and indirect strategies wins.

SUN TZU, *The Art of War* , 6th century BC

Yes sir, or rather *sir sci* .

In Mandarin this is the correct pronunciation of the last name of the Chinese president, Xi (Scì) Jinping. It is on the auspicious date of early spring, 21 March 2019, that the supreme leader receives a particularly respectful and solemn welcome on the occasion of his visit to Italy. There are some accompanying gaffes that only amuse Italians, such as that of the then Deputy Prime Minister Luigi Di Maio (future Foreign Minister) who reverses the traditional Chinese order, swaps his name and surname, calls him Jinping as if they were childhood friends . But the real focus is elsewhere. That day warning lights are lit in various European capitals, from Berlin to Paris, to Brussels; and a barrage of attacks comes from Washington.

Signor Sci , the Chinese president, is received with the honors due to the leader of the world's second superpower, heir to a millennial tradition. Nobody objects to the Italian deference. But there is something more, which puts the spotlights of the other Western governments on that visit: it is the signing, on March 23, of a Memorandum of Understanding, essentially an intergovernmental protocol which establishes the principles of a great understanding between Rome and Beijing. At the heart of the Memorandum is Italy's formal entry into the titanic Chinese Belt and Road project, i.e. "Belt and Road": what we know better as the New Silk Roads. In other words, the multiform roads of global interconnection in the third millennium: physical networks and digital networks, transport, energy, communications, a myriad of projects and constructions under Chinese direction.

Giuseppe Conte's Italy at that moment makes a symbolic gesture which is interpreted by some as a tear, by others as a leap in the dark. The tear is with its alliances: no other member country of the G7, none of the major nations of the European Union has yet made that gesture. None of the European and Western big names has agreed to formally enter into the plan with which Beijing "extends the tentacles" of its infrastructure and permanently annexes dozens of countries to its economy. What does Italy hope to achieve from this accession, exactly? In the immediate future, the Conte government on that March 23, 2019 is accused of serious imprudence, if not exactly of high treason, by America and its major European partners. Are they right or wrong? And was it worth it? Or this time "the trap" is the one that the Chinese have prepared for the Italians? Some already see the ports of Genoa and Trieste slipping towards Beijing's control; who points out that previously Chinese groups bought shareholdings in large Italian infrastructure operators such as Enel, Terna, Telecom Italia. Never mind the football clubs: those, by comparison, are local folklore. Much more crucial is the advance of Chinese capital in the nerve centers of energy and telecommunications.

Are we going to die Chinese, then? We Italians who were among the first users of the Silk Roads, with our traditions of trade towards the Levant, from the Roman Empire to the Republic of Venice and Marco Polo, will we end up sucked into the East, but this time in a subordinate position? Because one thing is clear. The Silk Roads of ancient history - on which spices and precious metals, ideas and religions also passed - had no master. Until the Renaissance and then the era of the great discoveries, many intermediaries operated along those lines, different peoples got rich thanks to those trades, nobody was the monopolist. From the ancient Romans to the Venetians, the role of our peninsula as a terminal of those communication routes was always important. So were many other intermediaries, from Persians to Indians, from Egyptians to Ethiopians, from Russians to Afghans. It's a fascinating story that I revisited in my book *The Red Lines* . But it is only today that the Silk Roads are being rediscovered, relaunched, upgraded and modernized by the overwhelming impulse of a nation. All roads led to Rome. Today they all end up in Beijing.

We do not exchange appearances and substance. In the Memorandum of Understanding between the People's Republic and our country there is no substantial concrete content, it is above all a statement of great principles, aspirations and projects, with the typical rhetoric of these documents. Trade deals and investments would be made anyway, regardless. Italy has left neither the EU nor NATO to suddenly become a Chinese colony. Not yet... the budgets will be made later. That text has a symbolic value. But symbols in foreign policy matter. Even more so when they are handled by a refined diplomacy that refers to millenary traditions, such as the Chinese one which now openly refers to continuity with the Celestial Empire.

So that March 23, Xi collected an obvious image success: Italy is a trophy, it is the first important western country that officially adheres to the Belt and Road plan, now the official name of the New Silk Roads (therefore from now on I will use the three terms interchangeably, with the sole purpose of avoiding annoying repetitions when reading). It must be remembered that a piece of this grandiose Chinese project was that Asian Investment Bank for Infrastructures against which Barack Obama already fought, who saw us as the first open challenge to the international order built by America starting in 1944, centered on multilateral institutions such as the International Monetary Fund, the World Bank, Gatt (later WTO, the World Trade Organisation).

Xi's China presents everything it does as a "win-win", a positive-sum game where everyone gains advantages. For example, in large infrastructural works two-way ties are strengthened: they can use the new rail and port, road and air networks to export even more easily; we can do the same by using them in reverse, to conquer new outlets on the Chinese market. Xi presents himself to us as the globalist of our time, with a positive vision of world trade, just as America retreats into sovereign isolationism. But is it really so? "Win-win," the win-win game, is a nice theory for economics textbooks. It requires a reciprocity of intents that does not exist. The Chinese market has a much older protectionist tradition than Trump's. It systematically discriminates in favor of its own national champions. This is all the more true in the titanic infrastructure construction sites that China opens all over the world, where opacity often reigns; companies from other countries are not treated as equals;

not to mention the problems of environmental sustainability, or workers' rights. Here is the first test to which Xi and his Memorandum must be subjected: what concrete and verifiable commitments does Beijing undertake to treat Italian interests fairly and with reciprocity?

Vigilance towards Xi does not mean absolving our partners' hypocrisies. Trump has bullied Europeans, he has not distinguished between allies and rivals, in fact he has made us all more vulnerable to Chinese expansionism. Germany, England and France, the Scandinavians, the Portuguese and the Balkans have welcomed more Chinese investments than us; sometimes they sold fine pieces of family silverware to Beijing. The risk of a Chinese semi-monopoly in fifth generation mobile telephony (Huawei) has been overlooked in Berlin and London. Now some are taking the chair and issuing belated and hypocritical warnings to Italy.

Xi is the only one who has very clear ideas. He is the first president since Mao who openly theorizes the superiority of his authoritarian model over our liberal democracies. Is it also this vision of the world that passes along the arteries of the New Silk Roads?

But what are we talking about when we use these terms: New Silk Roads or Belt and Road? The first was already in vogue in Beijing when I lived there: under the presidency of Hu Jintao, over a decade ago a real "conquest of the West" was underway, in an ideological atmosphere that has some similarities with the colonization of the Far West at dawn of the United States. The construction sites that had modernized China, giving it eight-lane highways and bullet trains, mega-airports and port stopovers for container ships, were now sweeping across the border. Bulldozers and excavators, cranes and columns of trucks, cement mixers and power cables, pipelines and optical fibers were stretching from China to all neighboring countries, starting with Southeast Asia and Central Asia. Already in those early years of the millennium when I lived in Beijing, there were frequent summits that attracted leaders from Africa and the Middle East to the Chinese capital, and they too were offered construction sites and billionaire investments. Reference to the ancient Silk Roads was part of the official rhetoric ever since.

However, a leap in quality and size, ambition and visionary power took place on September 7, 2013. Xi Jinping took office in the presidency of the People's Republic for a year. That day he is visiting Astana, the capital of Kazakhstan. At his side is Kazakh President Nursultan Nazarbayev. Xi delivers a speech that we must consider a milestone: "More than 2100 years ago, under the Han Dynasty of western China, the emperor's representative, Zhang Qian, was twice sent to Central Asia to open the door to friendly contacts with the peoples here. Today, let us unite to build the Silk Road economic belt, a great cause that will benefit all people along these routes." It is in that speech that Xi uses the initiative's new official name, Belt and Road, for the first time.

And it is in that year that he begins to quantify investments: Beijing announces its intention to mobilize at least one trillion, that is one trillion, dollars for the set of investment projects that radiate towards Eurasia, with bifurcations and branches in the Indian Ocean, Persian Gulf and Mediterranean. Four years later, Xi will enshrine the Belt and Road Initiative (or BRI) in none other than the Constitution of the People's Republic. An almost unheard-of gesture, from our point of view. It is as if in the 1950s we Italians had included the Autostrada del Sole in the Constitution. Or, an even more appropriate comparison, it is as if the United States had added an amendment to its Constitution to enshrine the Marshall Plan and the reconstruction of Western Europe.

In short, it is clear that the first to want to underline the historical, geopolitical and strategic importance of the New Silk Roads is him, the strong man at the helm of China, the first leader of Beijing since the fall of the celestial dynasty which returns to have an "imperial" vision. And here I use the term in the ancient and modern sense at the same time. Xi's China is one of the last multi-ethnic empires in the traditional sense as it controls vast territories populated by subjugated ethnic groups (Tibet, Xinjiang, Mongolia). Instead, it is a postmodern empire in its idea of expansion based mainly on economic, technological and financial influence: it subjects Eurasia with its capitals, not with weapons. Finally, in the «win-win» idea there is continuity with the imperial past: China of the past millennia considered itself the center of the universe, surrounded by vassal states that it did not need to conquer because they were in a subordinate position, tributaries and respectful of power relations, of hierarchies.

The driving idea is the exportability of a model. The whole world has now had thirty years to see what the Chinese are capable of: they were underdeveloped, still suffering from "African" famines at the end of the 1950s; today they have highways, railways and airports that are much more modern than the American ones, they have telecommunications giants, they have more Internet users than the entire West, they have brought electricity, sewage and drinking water, hospitals, schools and universities to the most remote corners and poor of their country. Now they "offer" this ability to all of us. Starting with the less developed neighbors, to get to the old Europe afflicted by a long stagnation.

In order not to be generic, you have to look at the atlases, the geographical maps, and follow the progress of the Belt and Road projects along at least six directions, all starting from China. They call them "economic corridors".

The first is the continental corridor, known as the "new land bridge of Eurasia": it starts from the Chinese region of Xinjiang, crosses Kazakhstan and southern Russia. The second starts north of Beijing, in the former Manchuria area near the Korean border, and is the Mongolia-Russia corridor. The third, called "China - Central Asia - South Asia", travels through various former Soviet republics including Tajikistan and Uzbekistan (just like the Cameleers' and Marco Polo's Silk Roads, from Tashkent to Samarkand and Buckara), arrives in Iran via through Tehran, then it crosses all of Turkish Anatolia, Istanbul, the Balkans, and there it rejoins branches of the Russian corridor, as well as central Europe. The fourth corridor leads to the naval routes and from the large coastal metropolises of Shanghai, Fuzhou, Guangzhou it connects with the ports of Vietnam, Singapore, Indonesia. The fifth, still predominantly naval, touches the coasts of Myanmar (Burma) and Bangladesh. The sixth is the one that from Kolkata (Calcutta) crosses the Indian Ocean and heads for Kenya, the Horn of Africa, and from there it goes up towards the Suez Canal and the Mediterranean. The sixth corridor already extends up to the port of Athens (bought by the Chinese) and could have new branches with settlements in Genoa and Trieste.

The breadth, grandeur and complexity of the entire New Silk Roads project is dizzying. Along those six corridors there is a swarm of already built works, open construction sites or projects under discussion with local governments. To the large "physical" infrastructures that are very conspicuous to the naked eye, such as highways, bridges, airports, railways, ports, oil pipelines, power plants, are added those that are less visible, such as underground fiber optic lines, aqueducts and sewers; or the «smart cities» (intelligent cities), urban planning projects for the technological management of the metropolis (urban transport, roads, but also hi-tech surveillance and security against crime or terrorism). A "Chinese Internet" also travels along these lines, that is, a model of authoritarian control of the Web that many other illiberal regimes like.

In the first three years since Xi's announcement, the Belt and Road construction sites have already created 180,000 jobs. China has already benefited from this as its trade with the nations it crosses has exceeded $3 trillion.

It should not be thought that the programs for the New Silk Roads form part of a single plan, centralized and controlled in every detail by the Beijing government. Under that label there are very different realities. Some infrastructure projects were already underway before Xi took office, and were later reclassified into the Belt and Road to gratify him. There is a mix of public investments agreed at the highest level between governments, but also private initiatives promoted by large Chinese companies, which subsequently sought government support and funding. The extent of the interventions is such that it is impossible to catalog everything: the projects already completed and those in the making involve 70 countries where half of the world's population lives and where 40 percent of the planet's wealth and 75 percent of its energy resources are concentrated . If you add all the countries that have expressed interest and would like to be included in the Belt and Road, the total rises to 130 countries. The temptation to put everything inside that container means that recently its label has also been used to talk about the Chinese advance in the Arctic or in Latin America; and even the sale of Chinese trains for the subways of Boston, Chicago, Los Angeles.

There is no shortage of criticism, resistance, skepticism about the scope of the plan. A good synthesis is offered by an American expert, Eyck Freymann, of whom an essay will be published in 2020 whose title in Italian sounds like this: «The Emperor's new clothes: One Belt One Road and the globalization of Chinese power». In an anticipation on the Bloomberg website, Freymann defines the titanic Belt and Road as a simple marketing operation. He underlines the contradictions in the numbers: some speak of investment plans for 1,000 billion, some for 5,000, some even for 8,000 billion dollars: a vagueness that leads to suspicion. Neither the propaganda hyperbole of those who define it as a new Marshall Plan, or "the dawn of Eurasia", nor the alarmism of those who speak of "predatory diplomacy, a public debt trap" destined to exploit emerging countries with new forms of neocolonialism.

According to Freymann, the Belt and Road Initiative should be understood in the context of the reborn cult of personality, nurtured around his own figure by Xi. Since it was mentioned in the Constitution alongside Xi's name, that brand has been attached to the most disparate, sometimes unconnected, initiatives born even many years before its definition. Basically, anyone who wants to curry favor with the new emperor has an interest in joining the New Silk Roads. Chinese public and private companies, colossal or medium-sized, are competing to jump on the bandwagon by gluing Belt and Road on any project abroad, good or bad, old or new. This has inflated its size because so much of China's cross-border investment that would have happened anyway now seems to be driven by that grand vision. There is also no shortage of waste and inefficiency, or "cathedrals in the desert" (very expensive, pharaonic and useless projects like a twin of the Panama Canal to be built in Nicaragua, now abandoned), especially since the Belt and Road brand is a convenient shortcut for those wishing to apply to receive subsidized loans from Chinese public banks.

Finally, Freymann cites the most well-known objections, also advanced by some governments "benefited" by the apparent Chinese generosity. There is the problem of the public debt that Beijing is exporting along the famous six corridors. Major works are not given away, they are financed by loans, and when the receiving country fails to repay them, China repays itself by becoming the owner of important assets: it expropriates land, mines and local companies from the insolvent debtor. Some of these countries, such as Pakistan, came close to bankruptcy and were forced to ask for help from the International Monetary Fund, which was ignorant of their financial crisis, because Chinese credit is not transparent, it is not declared, it is invisible on screens radar of supervisory institutions. Like a debt-exporting machine, along the corridors of the Belt and Road, China is transferring its development model based on borrowed capital and banking "bubbles" to many emerging nations.

There is a systematic nationalist favoritism whereby the great works of the Silk Roads are mainly assigned (89 per cent) to Chinese companies, while the rest remain the crumbs (7.6 per cent to local companies, 3.4 per cent to third parties). The same goes for the use of manpower: too often Chinese workers work on construction sites, so those investments do not create as much employment as they should in the host countries. Moreover, one of the motives that seem to have motivated the famous six corridors from the outset is the need that China has to use its excess production capacity. The People's Republic produces too much steel and too much cement; it has an over ten-year speculative bubble in the construction sector, it has built too much, even entire ghost towns where the buildings are empty. Exporting construction sites throughout Asia, Africa, Europe and Latin America means using plants, equipment and manpower that would otherwise be unused. But the standards to which we Westerners are held - workers' rights, environmental impact - do not apply if the works are managed by Beijing.

In many cases, it is still the People's Republic that maintains operational control, and even ownership titles, over the large infrastructural networks already built or under construction. Expanding from the great industrial and financial centers of Beijing, Tianjin, Nanjing, Shanghai, Guangzhou on the coastal strip, Chongqing and Chengdu on the inner strip, the network of infrastructures that envelops Central Asia and then branches out towards Africa or the 'Europe already contains management know-how. China provides a new global model of large turnkey networks; but some keys he keeps. It is evident that together with optical fibers, telecom and wi-fi networks, Xi also offers the authoritarian regimes of emerging countries a competence relating to control of the Internet. China has now demonstrated that it can be at the same time a very technologically advanced nation, making extensive use of the potential of the Internet, but without suffering the contagion of the ideas that the West deluded itself into propagating on the Net. The model of a sophisticated Net, great multiplier of economic opportunities (from online commerce to digital payment systems) yet substantially forbidden to the American digital giants and their social media, it is very attractive to illiberal democracies, or democrats.

The criticisms listed by Freymann and other Americans are partly right, partly exaggerated. To discredit the Belt and Road as a simple marketing operation is frankly excessive: the World Bank itself, which is cut off from those Chinese projects, recognizes that of the 1,000 billion dollars promised by Beijing, as many as 575 (more than half) have already been spent or allocated. After all, it is enough to go around Central Asia or Africa to see the Chinese shipyards at a glance. During a long journey through Ethiopia in January 2019, I saw airports, roads, aqueducts and railways built by the Chinese: where they have not yet arrived, I saw girls and boys walking tens of kilometers on dirt roads or dusty paths , carrying water cans on his back. As for Europe: the non-stop rail link from China to Poland has already been completed, from where the trains continue on the entire continental network.

The problems encountered by Xi Jinping in his global advance are real, though. Starting with that of debt. Sri Lanka has truly fallen into a trap: failing to repay the Chinese credit installments for the construction of a new port (all carried out by Chinese companies), it had to sell it for 99 years to a large public company in Beijing. Thus Sri Lanka has become a negative model and a warning to all the other states: those who accept funds from Xi Jinping must know the risks they are exposed to; the yielding of sovereignty is not an abstract hypothesis. Pakistan, after coming close to sovereign bankruptcy and after obtaining a $6 billion bailout from the IMF in May 2019, has had to cut, downsize or postpone some of the Chinese projects at home. Myanmar has drastically reduced a Chinese-made port plan that would have cost $7.3 billion (it's brought it down to $1.3 billion). Malaysia has completely canceled a network of pipelines that China wanted to build there by investing 3 billion dollars, and has given up on building two-thirds of the new railway lines sponsored by Beijing. Kenya has stopped the construction of a Chinese power plant on the island of Lamu, a tourist destination that risked being deserted by visitors due to pollution, due to environmental impact problems. In Zambia it is the local workforce that has revolted against the oppressive methods of the new Chinese masters in the copper mines. Even the small Maldives has rejected Xi's offers, after uncovering numerous cases of corruption.

Criticism and resistance, however, did not go unnoticed in Beijing. Official Chinese propaganda perhaps attributes them to Washington's *long arm* , denounces plots by American imperialism, accuses Westerners of being envious. In fact, the leaders of the People's Republic take note of the problems encountered and try to correct the mistakes. At a Belt and Road forum convened in Beijing in April 2019, Xi Jinping announced that his government will exercise more control over the quality of projects, and will be selective and vigilant even in the execution phases. He promised environmentalism and a crackdown on corruption. Even on the question of debts, he guarantees greater caution; in an exemplary gesture, a railway project in East Africa, from Mombasa to Nairobi, to Uganda and beyond, was canceled to avoid overloading already over-indebted Kenya with another $5 billion in loans.

Another of the lessons that Xi Jinping learned from those mishaps concerns us. Among the course corrections made by Beijing in the strategy on the New Silk Roads, there is a shift of attention towards already developed countries. Russia has become an increasingly important partner, also as a result of the strategic understanding between Xi and Putin. Italy's signing of the Memorandum, which follows the accession of smaller European countries (from Portugal to the Balkans), is the confirmation of an adjustment of fire. The six corridors will continue to swarm with construction sites, but the center of gravity shifts, the excessive weight of the debts of poor countries is balanced by diverting investments towards industrialized areas. Europe becomes the most prized loot also because it is a deposit of know-how and technological knowledge that Chinese companies can draw on.

Ultimately it would be wrong to underestimate the Belt and Road, to focus only on errors, atrocities or propaganda exaggerations. There is an alternative reading.

A Marshall Plan on steroids. A more modern and less expensive strategy of alliances than the military projection of the US armed forces on a planetary scale. One way to overcome the role of the Strait of Malacca as a «jugular» which can be narrowed in the event of an American-China conflict. These are the most positive interpretations of the Belt and Road Initiative. I find them in the essay by a researcher of Indian origin, Sarwar Kashmeri, *China's Grand Strategy. Weaving a New Silk Road to Global Primacy* , published in 2019 in New York by the Foreign Policy Association. The parallel with the Marshall Plan is striking. It was the economic premise and the social glue on which NATO was to rest: the consensus towards the hegemony of the United States was built on aid which facilitated post-war reconstruction and triggered thirty years of progress.

Today China has to face an America that continues to have an overwhelming military superiority: Beijing's spending on arms is a third of Washington's, at least officially. But the People's Republic does not try to compete on an equal footing: building the equivalent of US fleets led by 11 nuclear aircraft carriers (each of which, alone, is the flagship of firepower greater than that of many sovereign states) would be a long and expensive pursuit. On the one hand, Beijing is pursuing an asymmetric warfare strategy which, with lighter investments, has already made its coasts unassailable. On the other hand, its counter-network of alliances is being built with the New Silk Roads.

The comparison with the American model based on formal treaties of alliance (with Japan and South Korea, or with the European partners of the Atlantic Pact) is misleading. The economy, commerce, infrastructures can create a community of interests just as solid as formal treaties. The Shanghai Group, which unites China, Russia and the former Soviet republics of Central Asia, is an example of this approach. China's investments through the Belt and Road scream neocolonialism, but the same kind of protests arose in Western European anti-American circles about the Marshall Plan.

The other interesting aspect of the BRI is the string of land-based infrastructure that runs across Central Asia, from Pakistan to Kazakhstan, promising to reduce China's dependence on supertankers plying the Strait of Malacca. That naval passage is the jugular vein that the American military fleet could choke, bringing the People's Republic to its knees in the event of conflict. So far, a scenario in which the Americans blockade the Strait of Malacca with their ships is deadly for China, which would run out of energy. In the future, that passage near Singapore may not be so vital anymore. The China-Pakistan corridor would reduce the distance from the Middle East to China from the current 12,900 kilometers (sea) to just 3,000 (land). Kashmeri, who grew up in Mumbai, notes that his native India, while not formally joining the BRI for political reasons, is also a major beneficiary of those Chinese investments.

Let us dwell on the comparison with the Marshall Plan, launched by the American president Harry Truman to finance the reconstruction of Europe devastated by the Second World War. Even in that case there were clauses of national preference: the recipient countries of the aid, such as Italy, had to use it mainly to buy industrial plants and machinery made in the USA. And even in that case there were forms of political interference, such as the use of loans to export an ideological model: Prime Minister Alcide De Gasperi led the Christian Democrats to victory in 1948 against the Social-Communist Front also because the Americans guaranteed him a credit of 100 million dollars, a "taste" of the economic benefits to come, if Italy had joined the Atlantic Pact.

The total aid offered to Europe with the Marshall Plan from 1948 to 1952, again in the form of loans, amounted to 13 billion at the time, which is the equivalent of about 110 billion dollars today. A cost that some American politicians and some of their constituents considered excessive. But today the dense network of economic relations that link the two sides of the Atlantic is worth 5,500 billion in annual trade and generates 15 million jobs. In short, it was a good investment for the United States to save Europe from hunger, from ruin, from a relapse into extremism and totalitarianism. Today's America – not just because of Donald Trump – seems to have lost both the will and the capacity for these great very long-term plans. China, on the other hand, thinks on broad horizons: some of Xi's programmatic declarations even project themselves up to the centenary of the foundation of the People's Republic, in 2049. A Western politician who proposed thirty-year projects to his constituents would be taken for a fanatic, and mocked by consequence. But basically, when America was in its ascendant phase it did just that.

President Franklin D. Roosevelt, even before having concluded and won the Second World War, with the Bretton Woods conference in 1944 laid the foundations of a system of economic and financial rules that would govern the world order for seventy-five years: Pax American, primacy of the capitalist economy, gradual opening of markets, in the context of networks of alliances and cooperation between liberal democracies. When Obama realized that China was creating the first brick of an alternative system - the Asian Infrastructure Investment Bank - he was able to react in no other way than by imploring his allies not to join. Few listened to him. All the major European nations have accepted Beijing's invitation and now have one foot in each of the two universes, the American-centric and the Sino-centric. Germany, France and the United Kingdom had already «betrayed» before us. Giuseppe Conte's signing of the Memorandum with China is just one of many episodes, in a progressive shift.

I return to the analysis of the American-Indian Sarwar Kashmeri, because he has an interesting theory on the "learning curve" of Chinese leaders. «The criticisms of the Road and Belt Initiative» he writes «are serious and embarrassing obstacles. But China can learn a lot from these growing pains by continuing to push ahead with its plans. After all, China has only ten years of Belt and Road experience; it has less than thirty years under its belt in its new role as global superpower. He has a lot to learn. But it has already demonstrated a rare ability to make sensational changes when the national interest requires it: for example, the 180-degree conversion from a communist to a capitalist economy. And so, in a few decades, when a large part of the New Silk Roads will be built, many beneficiary nations will realize that it was not the West that gave them the infrastructures and tools for economic success, the West that preaches the values of democracy. It must have been China that won the approval of much of the world, the old-fashioned way: by earning it.

To the learning curve that describes Kashmeri I add this non-secondary detail. Given its huge - and problematic - involvement in Pakistan, China has had to force its companies to hire firms specializing in counter-terrorism security. The attacks on Chinese workers and managers have become a side effect of the New Silk Roads. Just as America in its imperial phase had to get used to facing forms of revolt or anti-American hostility in every corner of the planet, today it is up to China to grapple with these costs of power. The state agency that manages the Chinese electricity grid, as it is building power stations and pylons throughout Pakistan, has had to invest in paramilitary training of its employees. Who, before leaving Beijing, undergo anti-terrorism training courses, organized by the same national police academy. Here's an example of "growing pains." It is also interesting that Pakistan, an Islamic theocracy in the grip of a fundamentalist drift, protector of Osama Bin Laden as well as of the jihadist commandos of the Mumbai massacre, has opened its arms wide to a China that holds a million Uyghur Muslims in concentration camps . Realpolitik on both sides; after all, there were also numerous contradictions within the Pax Americana, when in the West there was room for the dictatorships of Franco in Spain, Salazar in Portugal and Pinochet in Chile.

I have two conflicting impressions from my trip to Ethiopia. On the one hand, gratitude to the Chinese, bearers of paved roads which are a precondition for freeing oneself from poverty. It's too easy to take them for granted when you live in a rich country. Paving a road makes the difference for millions of children in the daily commute from home to school – which without modern transport can take many hours, with all the dangers involved, not least the serial rapes of girls on long, solitary journeys – and helps to avert illiteracy trap. On the other hand, many Ethiopians are concerned about Chinese intrusion but do not have a solid Western alternative to limit it.

The balance sheets on the New Silk Roads will be made in the long term, if not exactly in 2049. This also concerns Italy's role: will it have been able to seize Chinese investment opportunities without giving up pieces of national sovereignty? We will be reminded of Washington's severe condemnation of the signing of the Memorandum on the Belt and Road: "That initiative was made by China for China," warned the National Security Council then headed by

John Bolton, "it excludes benefits for the Italian people and could damage the country's economic reputation.

Even on this titanic project to connect ever more closely every corner of the planet - and the rest of the world to China - weighs the shadow of the new cold war, which could force everyone to choose sides. Certainly the appeal of the Western camp has diminished in direct proportion to our disengagement from so many areas of the world. Those who for decades had shouted " *Yankee Go Home* " in the square , who had denounced the interference and intrusiveness of Uncle Sam, today expose themselves to the famous American proverb " Be careful what you *wish for* ". best wishes», because there is a risk that it will come true. And those who wanted to see only waste, corruption, robbery, neocolonialism in our cooperation funds and development aid will now realize what it means to leave those spaces empty: someone else has already filled them in.

V

African factory, western retreat

In the year 762 AD, Du Huan in Guangzhou writes a book, the *Jingxingji* or Travel Diary. One of the excerpts from that text that survived in a Chinese encyclopedia tells of a land, Molin, whose inhabitants were black. No rice or grain, no grass or trees grew. The horses were fed dried fish. In inland regions, diarrhea was treated with skull incisions. ... Molin corresponded to the coastal areas of Eritrea and Sudan.

FRANÇOIS-XAVIER FAUVELLE, «The tribulations of two Chinese in East Africa», in *The Golden Rhinoceros* (Einaudi, 2017)

Gabriele Delmonaco is Italian but lives in New York, where he directs an American humanitarian NGO, A Chance in Life. He was my guide on my trip to Ethiopia in January 2019. There we visited NGO-funded country schools and hospitals. More recently, he told me about this discovery of his. For the children it assists in Ethiopia, A Chance in Life used to buy clothes, shoes and school overalls, naturally on site and mainly from an American brand, Children's Place, whose clothing items are widespread in the country and are cheap. Although he tried to help the local economy with his purchases, Delmonaco regularly discovered that the products were made in China. The American brand, like many others, entrusted its production to Chinese subcontractors with long-term contracts. Only recently, for the first time, Children's Place sold him goods made right there in Ethiopia.

Other testimonies from Africa confirm that it is not an isolated case. One explanation is Donald Trump's tariffs, which accelerate the new relocations: the same Chinese textile-clothing giants transfer production to countries where labor costs even less, and above all they are not affected by American customs taxes. I knew about Vietnam and Bangladesh; now the relocation of factories also benefits African states, first and foremost Ethiopia. In theory, these countries should be grateful to American protectionism, but it is an indirect, distant, complicated cause to understand. What the Africans see is the reality they face: it is the Chinese subcontractors who bring them work.

The African continent exceeds the United States, China, India and Europe combined by extension. It has over 1.2 billion inhabitants - almost as many as China today - but given its birth rates will more than double, 2.5 billion, in 2050. Long before then, already in five years, household consumption of middle class populations will exceed 2 trillion dollars a year.

Africa, writes Indian-American economist Sarwar Kashmeri, "is set to become the greatest economic opportunity in history since China's transition to capitalism." And who will be the co-protagonist of this transition? We know the answer will be China. We have been talking about its advance in the Black Continent for years, with stereotypes that have now entered bar conversations: «The Chinese are buying Africa, they are its new masters, they are invading it to plunder its raw materials». All of this is true, and is already arousing protests or resistance from segments of the population and local ruling classes. But if we don't go further, if we stop at those clichés with which we liquidate the sinicization of Africa, the historical significance of what is happening escapes us. The challenge between China and the West will largely hinge on the fate of Africa. And in fact we have decided that we are not interested in having a role. The attitude of Westerners – even those who think they are "humanitarian" – consists in standing by and watching. Profound changes are happening in the interaction between Chinese and Africans, with Americans and Europeans busy criticizing from afar.

Irene Yuan Sun is only 32 years old and already has an outstanding resume. Born in China, she left it when she was 6 when her parents moved to America. He did brilliant studies, up to Harvard University. She has never stopped caring about her home country, though: she worked at the McKinsey company as an expert on Chinese investments in Africa; today she is a researcher in a think tank in Washington, the Center for Global Development. He wrote a beautiful and important book, *The Next Factory of the World* (Harvard Business Review Press, 2017), that is «the next factory of the world». It's nice because his life is also in it, many personal experiences (like his first job as a teacher in a middle school in Namibia); important, because it offers us an original point of view on the new "colonization" of Africa by China, forcing us to review our prejudices. It has not been translated into Italian, so I summarize some of its contents here.

The book begins with Irene Yuan Sun's childhood in China, and is startling from the very first lines.

I remember the first time I got into a car. Not many in America can say the same thing, cars are trivial. But it happened in China, where I was born and where I lived up to the age of six... I was used to holding my parents' hand tight, standing on a crowded bus; or clinging to them as they pedaled their bicycles... The car didn't belong to our family, of course. It was the early 1990s, and hardly anyone in China had a car. A family friend who was a government official gave us a tour, as a present... I want to point out that this was only twenty-five years ago. Young as I am, I lived in a China where the streets weren't crowded with cars like today but with bicycles... Since then, GDP has grown thirty-fold, and 750 million people have been lifted out of poverty. China had been poorer than Kenya, Lesotho, Nigeria... Today it competes with the United States for world supremacy.

Let us dwell on this last sentence, which could go almost unnoticed by a Western reader. But if you are a citizen of Kenya, Lesotho or Nigeria, it is an observation that leaves you baffled, dumbfounded; then it persecutes you: why did China, which was poorer than us, manage to do it? Is the Chinese model replicable? It is certainly the most gigantic, spectacular, perhaps the only one available at the moment, because India does not do the same for exports and showcases.

We also think of that terrible thing, rightly deprecated by us Westerners and also by some Chinese, which was the one-child policy. In its forced, authoritarian application, it has had horrendous human costs. At the same time it has prevented the birth of 300 or 350 million Chinese. Too many more mouths to feed, as they used to say when China was very poor. Those who see Africa as a demographic bomb must also ask themselves about this: what if one day Africans were able to imitate the Chinese recipe?

In the quarter century in which the economic boom is transforming her country, Irene Yuan Sun grows up as a teenager in the United States. After university, he goes to teach English and mathematics in a village in Namibia. The principal also entrusts her with another task: she has to take care of the management of the school shop. Since she's not sure which products to sell, at the end of a lesson she asks her pupils if anyone would like to take her to the wholesaler, which is an hour's drive away. By car. Open up heaven, all the girls and boys raise their hands shouting, everyone would like to go with her, some chase her around the house after class, begging her to accept them as escorts.

For me the scene was fun and familiar, I knew that desire to sit in a car, and the taste of the novelty of actually doing it. Cars, or Sprite, or toilet paper, may seem like very materialistic ways of defining development. Those who have always had these things tend to forget how much they are signs of modernity for those who don't have them.

(Yes, but why also Sprite? Because that sealed can is the guarantee of a drinkable drink, which does not poison, and gives energy with sugar.)

After months of teaching five middle school classes, Irene Yuan Sun feels frustrated, useless, or worse. His pupils are mostly children of poor peasants and most will in turn become poor peasants. She sees the absurdity of her job: she teaches the conjugations of English irregular verbs to girls and boys destined to cultivate small fields, in an arid plain where no one speaks English. Before his eyes he sees real tragedies unraveling - kids grappling with an AIDS epidemic, environmental degradation, misery - and he has nothing to offer to help them. The idea that education is the key to the future of those young people seems nonsensical to her.

Then a strange encounter happens to her. She gives in to pressure from a local Chinese acquaintance of hers and agrees to go on a *blind date* , a blind date with an aspiring boyfriend. Chinese too. Thirty years old, rich, desperately looking for a wife; few Chinese women are willing to emigrate to Africa. On the evening of the meeting, at dinner and after a few beers, she discovers that she is dealing with the typical Chinese businessman in Africa:

A pure capitalist, indifferent to the welfare or human rights of the local population. Yet I was struck by this: He could do more to help the people of the village than my well-intentioned efforts. I taught the children knowledge that was theoretically useful for a world in which none of them would ever live. He created real jobs and real wages.

The engagement does not take place, and that man Irene Yuan Sun will never meet him again. However, the shocking revelation she had in that meeting will push her to devote years to studying Chinese investments in Africa, to explore dozens and dozens of factories created by these capitalists, to interview their owners, employees, trade unionists, to hear all the versions possible about what is happening. That is, on what we call the invasion, the colonization, the imperialist advance of China in Africa. Yuan Sun has no preconceptions, he is not a priori in favor of the initiatives of his fellow countrymen. It exposes all the criticisms, all the fiercest or most disturbing aspects of reality. But he comes to a clear and positive conclusion:

Chinese factories in Africa, this is the future that will create widespread prosperity for Africans and open the next stage in global development. It will make Africa richer, with a substantial and lasting improvement in living standards.

Africa, recalls the young researcher, has been the experimental laboratory for waves of Western ideas on the fight against poverty. Aid programs from the West have certainly improved childhood education and brought about advances in health care (although never enough). But it will not be the aid culture dear to the West that will create the hundreds of millions of jobs needed to lift half a billion poor Africans out of poverty. More is needed, and this other is the factories. No part of the world, neither America nor Europe nor Asia, has been able to defeat atavistic poverty without going through some form of industrialization. And who is bringing oodles of factories to Africa? Especially them, our adversaries or rivals, the Chinese. Just twenty years ago, in the year 2000, only two Chinese investments in Africa were surveyed; today hundreds arrive a year.

A McKinsey study surveyed over 10,000 Chinese companies operating in Africa. Some produce for the local market, attracted for example by the purchasing power of Nigerian consumers: in 2050 Nigeria will have more inhabitants than the United States. Other Chinese companies, on the other hand, look to low labor costs and go to produce in Africa and then export elsewhere, perhaps to the West. The case I came across, that of Children's Place in Ethiopia, is just one example among many. In Lesotho, Chinese companies manufacture yoga suits for the Kohl brand, jeans for Levi's, sports shoes for Reebok: almost all of Lesotho's clothing and footwear production ends up on the American market.

"Industrialization is how China has transformed itself from a poor and backward nation to one of the largest economies on the planet in just thirty years. By becoming the next "factory of the world", Africa can do the same» writes Yuan Sun. On the dark side of this story, I always quote you because your analysis is lucid.

Let's be clear, the rise of the manufacturing sector is not all a happy story. Up close, it is often ugly. Some Chinese bosses in the factories I've visited are downright unpleasant. Racists. They do not hesitate to pay bribes. They get drunk, hang out with prostitutes, spit in public. Their corruption affects the functioning of local governments, the environmental impact of their factories affects air and water quality, their treatment of employees determines not only wage levels but sometimes even life or death on the work place. China itself – with corruption scandals and pollution at home – offers distressing examples of the consequences of wild economic development. Industrialization unleashes both destructive and positive forces, all of which is already visible in today's Africa.

The field research conducted by the scholar also invites us not to assume that China is "replicating" its model, as it is, in Africa. It would not be possible. For better or for worse, there will be an African version of the Chinese paradigm. Some African countries receiving Chinese investment have a free press, which does not exist in Beijing; others have strong unions, unheard of in Shanghai; many have tribal traditions that the People's Republic at home has swept away in its nationalist centralism. In the most pessimistic version, it is legitimate to doubt that the Chinese model will be replicated because Africa has neither the ancient entrepreneurial tradition (in China the first forms of capitalism date back to the thirteenth century) nor the collective discipline typical of a Confucian culture. It is far too early to tell what will emerge from the blend of capitalism from Beijing and the local conditions upon which it operates as it is transplanted into the African social fabric. It is a historic experiment of enormous significance, of which we are only observing the beginning, because it is still too recent.

It should be added that Yuan Sun deals with half of the story. He has explored the private and spontaneous part of the Chinese invasion, the same one which a colleague of the "New York Times" who was a bit Chinese and a bit African due to his professional experience and family ties, Howard French, became interested in years ago. He too went on the hunt for that unplanned entrepreneurial emigration from Beijing but rather messy, chaotic, driven by the thirst for adventure and profit. At least one million small Chinese entrepreneurs, traders, intermediaries in search of fortune have emigrated to

Africa in search of their New World; without asking permission from their government or receiving instructions or aid. A biblical exodus sometimes inspired by dissatisfaction with the motherland.

It is a kind of new "conquest of the West", because this human fauna reproduces the mentality of certain white settlers when they crossed America. Their interaction with the local population is much closer and more intense than the armies of managers and technicians of the large Chinese state-owned companies who go to build roads, skyscrapers and airports. These Chinese set out to conquer Africa in no particular order – but ready to show solidarity with their fellow men, to create networks of *guanxi* , between mutual aid and mafia fraternity – they do not obey a geopolitical plan but perhaps support it without knowing it. They are those of the «flying geese model», the image used by economists to describe waves of business migrations, which build up critical mass and transplant industrialization into new lands. They are people who have courage to sell, they leave behind their land and their ancestral ties, a millenary culture, and move to a continent of which they know nothing, let alone speak any of the local languages. The show is dizzying: it is the story of Africa entering a new phase. All of this is literally happening before our eyes: but we Westerners are just spectators. In many African countries, the ratio of Chinese to Western investment is ten to one.

The other half of the story is the one that is talked about most often. I also mention it in the chapter on the New Silk Roads. These are Chinese investments planned from above and agreed between governments, under the direction of Beijing and the protagonism of its large state companies. They mainly concern infrastructure. The criticisms against this Chinese macro-invasion – due to the environmental impact, corruption, the debts charged to local states, the exploitation of the workforce – have also been widespread in our media for years now. The list of monsters born from the Chinese advance is long. I recall here a couple of the most cited stories. There is the infamous $10 billion railway in Kenya. A first section of 500 kilometres, already built and in operation, connects the port of Mombasa and the capital Nairobi. A second one is almost completed. But the corruption surrounding that great work is such that the construction costs per kilometer are double the international average, while the cargo carrying capacity is only 40 percent of that promised. The project is so infamous that it has become something of an example of everything that can go wrong. The criticisms do not leave Xi Jinping indifferent, who is in part trying to correct course. In April 2019, when Kenyan President Uhuru Kenyatta paid an official visit to Beijing to solicit the financing of the last tranche, the Chinese government left him dry. They are sick of pouring billions into that bottomless pit. The last stretch of the railroad, which was supposed to reach Lake Victoria and has a budget of 3.5 billion dollars, may never be built.

Another famous scandal concerns Tanzania, where in 2013 the Chinese started planning a very modern container port in Bagamoyo, once a naval port for the slave trade, then reduced to a fishing village. This megaconstruction too had an estimated cost of 10 billion dollars, and disproportionate ambitions: the Chinese builders "projected" a future in which Bagamoyo would overtake the traffic of Rotterdam, number one among European airports. Most disturbing was the clause in which the Chinese reserved a 99-year lease as collateral for their loans. In June 2019, the President of Tanzania John Magufuli decided to block the permanent jobs, in order not to end up in the trap of the insolvent debtor whose house is being foreclosed.

The government of Sierra Leone has done the same with a controversial project to build an airport, always in fear of becoming a slave to the Chinese by dint of getting into debt with them. "The perception that there is a plot to turn the entire Indian Ocean into a Chinese lake is jeopardizing the political capital China has amassed among Africans," wrote The Economist . » on June 29, 2019. The same British magazine, however, cites a study by Johns Hopkins University in Baltimore, according to which projects overwhelmed by debts are a small minority out of 3,000 cases of large Chinese works abroad. Certainly the 50 most indebted countries to the People's Republic (many of which are African) have now accumulated an average of debts equal to 17 percent of their GDP, which is enormous as exposure to a single foreign creditor. But China has also had to learn – at its own expense – the "art of forgiveness": 140 times since 2000 it has had to reschedule and partly cancel credits to poor countries.

Perhaps it is more concerning to observe the advance of another kind of Chinese model in Africa, not railways and airports but censorship. In 2019 alone, six other African governments joined the list of those blocking the Internet to prevent freedom of expression and the circulation of inconvenient news. Social media like Facebook, Twitter, Instagram, WhatsApp are regularly blacked out. Some of these governments buy ready-made know-how "turnkey" from the large Chinese telecom companies, which are at the forefront of the world in this field.

However, the sinicization of Africa is not the meeting between two distant worlds as we believe, nor even less a very recent consequence of what we have defined globalization. It's actually a throwback. One of the greatest scholars of ancient African history, the Frenchman François-Xavier Fauvelle, reminds us that the first contacts between the Celestial Empire and African civilizations date back as far as the eighth century AD, under the Tang dynasty. More important for their influence were the explorations of Admiral Zheng He under the Ming dynasty, with two African missions, one in 1417-1419, the other in 1421-1422. His fleet landed in Somalia and Kenya. It is possible that she arrived in present-day South Africa and circumnavigated the Cape of Good Hope. Chinese art of the Ming period is full of references to Africa; Chinese handicrafts from the 15th century have been found on the African coast. The two worlds are old acquaintances, which reconnect ancient relationships in a brand new context.

The sinicization of Africa gets bad press in the West, but what alternative are we offering? We accuse Xi Jinping of invading the Dark Continent to grab its natural resources: agricultural crops, minerals. There is no doubt, China is hungry for raw materials for its industries. Furthermore, the People's Republic knows that one of its Achilles heels is nutrition. It does not have enough arable land to feed 1.4 billion people. It is suffering from a frightening water crisis, with desertification phenomena that climate change can only worsen. China invades Africa with the ancient mentality of a landowner and the modern mentality of someone buying a life insurance policy for the future. All the more in the context of the new cold war with the United States: access to the "breadbasket" of the Midwest becomes problematic. Soybeans and cereals, which Beijing has been importing from American farmers for decades, now have to look for them elsewhere. But for Africa this looting also means finding an outlet for its exports. For decades, African farmers had to sell coffee and cocoa to us Westerners at robbery prices; Chinese demand could improve their bargaining power a bit.

From what pulpit do we lecture and spread the alarm about Chinese colonization? We Westerners also went to Africa mainly to exploit its natural resources. We have left you, in return, nothing resembling the road and rail networks built by the Chinese today. France continues to maintain a real colonial army, troops that intervene regularly in Mali or in the Central African Republic: it is not as active as China in building infrastructure.

In Europe, Africa is spoken of as a black hole where nothing positive happens. For the European media it is a constant tragedy. Attention is focused on epidemics, civil wars and of course migratory flows, in particular of those seeking asylum on the northern shores of the Mediterranean. What is "behind" those refugees is evoked like a nightmare: the demographic bomb, precisely, the future two billion Africans who are described as a mass of desperate people ready to invade the Old Continent in an Apocalypse migratory.

These depictions distort our perception of Africa and its problems, and further distort our assessment of what we are doing for them. The media obsession with a few hundred asylum seekers trying to land in Italy, for example, focuses inordinate attention on microscopic numbers. The "humanitarian" model that wants open borders helps very few people and not the most needy: although desperate, and poor compared to us, those who can pay thousands of euros for a smuggling mafia are the result of an economic selection. They are, in reality, a privileged minority at home.

But the method adopted in "progressive" countries, from Canada to Germany to Sweden, which increasingly practices a government of migratory flows that selects on the basis of professional talent, is no better. Doctors or computer scientists, mathematicians or managers boast a title that candidates them for Canadian, German, Swedish visas and residence permits. This creams from Africa an elite that serves us; it is the classic emigration that permanently impoverishes the countries of departure. To date, 1.2 billion Africans need help in their homes; better yet: instead of being "helped", they need to be trained and hired by employers who use them to create local wealth. The Chinese are doing it. Not out of humanitarian generosity, but out of sinister interest and for the purpose of profit. Capitalism "is not a gala party", to paraphrase Mao Zedong (who spoke of the revolution). It worked spectacularly in China, though. Those hundreds of millions of Chinese who risked starvation were not saved by the concerts of progressive rock stars or by non-profit fundraisers. With all due respect to the precious work of aid workers, the Chinese miracle was done by the Chinese themselves, with sweat, toil and sacrifices, after having been freed from a disastrous economic ideology and authorized to get rich.

Only the snobbery of Westerners who already have everything - and therefore yearn for "happy degrowth" - can fail to see that the great story of our time is this: will China succeed in getting Africa off the ground by putting Africans to work, where we have failed over and over again?

If China succeeds with its "ugly, dirty and bad" recipe, this is a scenario that could also change the fate of the new cold war. Can we imagine a future in which only we Westerners will be left to oppose Chinese expansionism – afflicted by stagnation, aging, divided and undecided about everything – while Africa will side with China? What a trap indeed.

VI

Italy at the crossroads

Will we die Chinese? Might we just resign ourselves, take some advantage of our slow slide under a new imperial hegemony? Or, instead, will we have to unite in defense of Western values, with a clear choice of sides, raising barriers and siding with America? The great geopolitical scenarios are closer and more concrete than we think. We are already faced with difficult choices, with enormous consequences. Here and now, Italy (like all of Europe) is contested between the two superpowers. One port at a time, one technology company at a time, one stock exchange or cell tower at a time, the America-China race invades every square kilometer of our territory. We are at stake.

Everything I have been dealing with on an intercontinental scale for decades takes on a familiar, local dimension, in my mother's city. Genoa is a special observatory for understanding how China moves its pawns, how rapidly it is advancing in our house, which strategic sectors it wants to conquer. A hill with a sea view, named Erzelli, is the starting point for my exploration. At the Erzellis there is the headquarters of the Italian Institute of Technology which deals with robotics, surrounded by leading companies in the biomedical, IT and telecom sectors. It is also a viewpoint overlooking the port of Genoa, the infrastructure that connects Europe, Northern Italy, the Mediterranean. On all these realities, Chinese ambition has become pressing; in some cases we are well beyond the expressions of interest. China is already here as the owner, perhaps without our knowledge.

The Italian Institute of Technology (Iit), to begin with, is a small Silicon Valley in our house. It is an excellence recognized throughout the world, even surprising in a city like Genoa, which too often has been synonymous with decadence, or even tragedy with the collapse of the Morandi bridge. 1,700 researchers work at the Iit. A third are foreigners, who have come from every corner of the planet, including America. 16 percent are «returning brains», young Italian talents who were previously expatriates and have now found an opportunity in their native country. At the Iit, these researchers work in leading sectors such as life sciences (biogenetics), nanomathematics, artificial intelligence, the supercomputers of the future. Just like in Californian universities – for example Stanford, which is in the heart of Silicon Valley – the IIT combines pure research and entrepreneurial applications: it has already given birth to twenty start-ups, company shoots. Such a business incubator and nursery of innovations attracts multinationals: Siemens, Ericsson, Nikon have established themselves in Erzelli and its surroundings; others are coming. There are large public bodies such as the European Space Agency that commission teams of young scientists to work.

The foreign equivalents of this Italian center are called the Massachusetts Institute of Technology (Mit) or the University of California. The comparison must be made with caution and humility; it doesn't hold up if we look at the size. The Iit lives on a budget of 125 million euros, mostly Italian and European public funds. MIT has ten times as much funding, the University of California (split across ten campuses including UC Berkeley, Los Angeles, San Diego, Santa Barbara and Santa Cruz) spends twenty times as much. However, the Iit uses those American samples as a reference standard for the rigor of its publications. It has hiring rules copied from Harvard. The evaluations of the candidates are entrusted to international commissions where none of the examiners has relations with the Iit. Absolute independence, the barriers against conflicts of interest, serve to avoid those self-referential mechanisms that often pollute Italian universities (nepotism, the logic of clans, recommendations, all things that made many talented young people flee abroad). At the Iit, the "permanent position" does not exist, for anyone. But when foreign or Italian candidates see the quality of the laboratories, they give up without hesitation on safer careers.

During a visit to the IIT in September 2019, I got a taste of the exciting frontiers of research in this Italian hub; and how they cross the Chinese question. Even a non-expert like me, who sometimes struggles to follow the language of the experts, gets excited. Nanomedicine is being worked on in the heights of Genoa, which allows the drug to be transported exactly into the microenvironment of the human body in which it must act: it is evident how this can reduce the need to "bombard" us with high doses of medicines with unwanted side effects or even dangerous, a bombardment only necessary until we can more accurately deliver the drug to a specific point in the body. Another laboratory on campus deals with a futuristic material, graphene. It is the thinnest thing that exists in nature, a sheet of graphene has the thickness of an atom. It is stronger and more flexible than steel, has prodigious qualities as an electrical and thermal conductor. It was only isolated by scientists in 2004. Someone compares the discovery-production of graphene to what the advent of aluminum was like: between 1796 and 1830 it allowed waves of technological and industrial innovations, from the Benz engine to the Wright brothers' planes . Will a graphene paint that releases heat perhaps one day replace radiators and heating systems in our buildings? Conjectures aside, we are just beginning to understand the potential of a material that could open up new horizons for energy saving and environmental protection.

In another department of the IIT, I was introduced to the world of iCubs, "baby robots", small humanoid machines or centaurs, quadrupeds with a human body or nearly so. A line of these iCubs is conceived and trained for emergencies: they have to replace us to intervene in the event of landslides, earthquakes, fires, floods, terrorist attacks. The aim is to save lives, including those of the police, firefighters, civil protection, all those who rush for the first interventions in the event of a disaster and risk ending up in the death toll. Anyone who watched the TV series *Chernobyl* will remember the episode where the Soviet authorities hope to be able to use robots for the most terrible work near the exploded nuclear reactor. Unfortunately, the robots of that generation - we are in 1986 - succumb to the shock of atomic radiation, are paralyzed and become useless. In their place, "human robots" are sacrificed, soldiers sent into jeopardy on a deadly mission due to the very high doses of radioactivity absorbed. Thirty-three years later, some of the iCubs being worked on in Genoa should be able to absorb high radiation doses. We hope that an accident like Chernobyl will never happen again, but there is much more work to be done, for example the decommissioning of nuclear power plants which are gradually being closed down.

Other teams of researchers are working on the "circular economy", the image coined to describe not only the recycling and reuse of technical materials, but also the separate collection of organic ones: the idea of circular economy evokes a sort of environmental balance permanent. I have seen biomedical applications that start from wool and silk waste from the textile industry or from algae and extract essential proteins to prepare "smart plasters", capable of releasing a drug into the skin and dissolving as the patient recovers. Or organic materials that absorb oil and other pollutants from the sea. On display are the organic alternatives to plastics: the world of industrial packaging, up to the packaging of fruit and vegetables in supermarkets, will be revolutionized by materials based on banana peels, orange peel, leftovers from the coffee machine. Nothing is created, nothing is destroyed, the new frontiers of sustainability are in these laboratories where a very young generation of scientists works, some of whom have "returned" from America.

Does all this have to do with China? Of course yes. A jewel like the IIT has not gone unnoticed on the other side of the world. One of the symbolic companies of this hi-tech Genoa, Esaote, has already ended up in the hands of a Chinese owner: at the forefront of Made in Italy biomedical, for example the production of equipment for ultrasounds, magnetic resonance imaging. In this case there was an acquisition by a private Chinese entity, which with Esaote "oversees" the Erzellis and thus set foot on the technological campus. In these parts there is growing interest from Tencent, one of the national champions on which Xi Jinping is betting. Tencent is the «T» in the acronym Bat, together with Baidu and Alibaba: they are the equivalent of Apple Amazon Google, the digital giants that have built dominant positions in China and expelled the Americans. The activism of Huawei, the telecom giant that has become the bete noire of the Trump administration, has also increased. As I write, the inauguration of a new Huawei branch in Genoa is imminent. There will be a significant volume of hiring, the Chinese are keen to let it be known that their impact will be beneficial on the city and regional economy. Local government authorities have already been approached, well in advance, for their political "blessing" of the company's official arrival. All this is happening while Washington is trying to draw a cordon sanitaire around Huawei, inviting allies to unite, in an operation to isolate and boycott 5G telephony "made in China".

The leaders of the Iit tell me of a China "very visible in the field of robotics, or on new materials such as graphene". They note that "for some years some of the main world conferences on robotics and artificial intelligence have been held in Shanghai, Beijing, Hong Kong, Macao". They add that «the Chinese Academy of Science is now the number one for high-level scientific publications in the sectors in which we operate». The Chinese often knock on the doors of the IIT to propose collaborations, "but the less we tell the Americans the better, as things are going on". A center of excellence in scientific research like the IIT feels the premonitory winds of the new cold war blowing. You have to move carefully. It is a public institution and most of its funds come from our Ministry of Economy, followed by the European Union. Everything that happens on the Erzelli hill runs the risk of being interpreted as Italy choosing sides in the US-China bipolar confrontation.

The sliding of the world towards the logic of blocks, of alignments, is even more evident when from the heights of the Erzelli I descend towards the sea. There was much talk of the port of Genoa as an object of Chinese desire, when Xi Jinping visited Italy and the first Conte government agreed to join the Belt and Road project by signing an official Memorandum (March 23, 2019). That document contained «memoranda of understanding» on the ports of Genoa and Trieste. Of all Italy's riches, maritime infrastructure is the one that arouses the most immediate appetite. The reason is clear, shipping is vital for a superpower that has built its wealth on foreign trade. China is a major exporter and also a voracious importer (for example of oil, cereals, soybeans, meat). Historically, some Silk Roads flow into the Mediterranean, a "corridor" that Chinese goods have used since ancient Roman times. The People's Republic cannot run the risk that the climate of a new Cold War will preclude some shipping lanes, or that certain foreign ports will suddenly become inaccessible to it following some form of embargo. These are extreme scenarios, political fiction for now. But whoever governs Beijing must take them into consideration.

Pax Americana worked as long as the United States assumed the privilege, responsibility, and burden of ensuring freedom of navigation on all oceans. The globalization dominated by America has offered many other nations the benefits of an open, accessible, fluid world. But if we enter a phase where America reverses its perception of the benefits of openness, if the winds of protectionism herald lasting change, then the Chinese need to fix it. Their penetration into port infrastructures serves that purpose. Precisely for this reason, when Conte signed the Memorandum with Xi and the ports of Genoa and Trieste appeared in that document, the alarm was immediately raised in Washington. In addition to the formal condemnations for Italy's entry into the Silk Road, informal pressures have multiplied. My Genoa, already accustomed to being a commercial crossroads, has also become a hot frontier for geopolitics, with close visits from American diplomats and Chinese ministers. This was not expected. There are cities that have already had the destiny of being "red lines", borders between empires: in the last cold war this role in Europe fell to Berlin, Vienna, Helsinki. In the next challenge between empires, not only Genoa and Trieste but the whole of Italy, as a bridge over the Mediterranean, could perform a similar function.

«The Chinese» the highest port authorities tell me, asking me for discretion «have understood that they are in the spotlight. Their every move suffered extreme visibility. Therefore, after the stage of ceremonies and treaties, they have adopted a pragmatic attitude and a lower profile. Given the alarm that their incursions into Italy arouse in Washington, they have learned their lesson and have begun to invite us to their homes. The new forms of Chinese hospitality are interesting. The Port Authority which governs the port of Genoa has been offered cooperation operations in some ports of China, participation in local logistics activities. The attraction is also strong because the Chinese are now at the forefront of e-commerce worldwide, and we certainly have something to learn by going to study them at home. With this offensive of seduction, Xi tries to show us that his promises are true: Belt and Road is a "win-win" operation, of mutual benefit, where we too have something to gain.

As for China's penetration into our ports, those who discovered the issue only with the Conte-Xi agreement of March 2019 are at least a decade late. The Chinese have already launched their bridgeheads in Italy, penetration is a deep-rooted reality. We need to look at Genoa not as a city, but as the head of a larger port system that includes the Savona area. On that stretch of the Ligurian coast, several ports of call compete. Of greatest interest to the Chinese are those equipped for container ships, where the loading and unloading of cargo takes place carrying the Global Box, the standardized metal parallelepiped, which travels on water, rail, highway, passing from ship to train to truck in a fast flow, from production to distribution. In the Vado Ligure container yard, the Chinese are already semi-owners, with 49 percent of the capital and in partnership with the Danish giant Maersk. For their other activities as shipowners they have a local company as a partner: the Cosulichs, who in their family history have their roots in Dalmatia and Trieste, in the ports of the Austro-Hungarian empire, even if today they have their headquarters in Genoa. The port of Vado is a terminal capable of receiving and handling (transferring them to other destinations) as many as 900,000 containers a year.

But nearby, another Asian power owns an even bigger port. The port of Voltri-Prà manages the transit of 2.5 million containers a year. It is in the hands of the Port Authority of Singapore, the small city-state which is a true superpower in the maritime sphere. Singapore is an interesting case for many reasons. First of all because it was an area of "African" misery until the early 1960s, then it became the protagonist of the most clamorous of Asian miracles. Today it is a very modern technopolis with one of the highest per capita incomes on the planet. This miniature dragon lives at home in a situation similar to that of Italy and Europe. The dilemma of the new cold war – «which side to be on» – arises in a much more pressing way in Singapore. China is geographically close to it, furthermore in the multi-ethnic composition of the metropolis it is the Chinese who have played a dominant role with the political founder of the city-state, Lee Kuan Yew. The other main ethnic groups are Malays and Indians; the official language is English, so as not to show favoritism towards this or that ethnic group.

Chinese Communist leaders have always admired and imitated Singapore's authoritarian Confucianism; it is a right-wing version of the model they aspire to ("meritocracy plus technocracy plus authoritarianism"). But precisely in order to have an insurance policy against China's excessive proximity, the Singaporean government has always been a friend of the United States, above all from a military point of view. With a subtle balancing act Singapore has managed in the past to have excellent relations with both Washington and Beijing. This has allowed for the growth of a shipping business where Singapore is a global giant, investing in Western ports without ever being met with the suspicions and reservations surrounding the Chinese. For decades, no one objected to Singapore becoming a sort of Switzerland of Southeast Asia – including its role as a tax haven – but the test by fire may still be ahead. To get an idea of its importance in global infrastructure and logistics, in addition to Savona, the Port Authority of Singapore is a shareholder of the ports of Antwerp (Belgium) and Gdansk (Poland). In terms of infrastructure, let us remember that the center of gravity of Europe - since the time of the discovery of the New World - has shifted clearly to the north, in favor of the Atlantic ports. The numbers recorded in Genoa are small compared to Rotterdam: the Dutch port handles 14.5 million containers a year. And all of Europe disappears in the face of the overwhelming superiority of Asia: it is in Singapore that they are building what will be the largest port in the world, 60 million containers a year. More than quadruple of Rotterdam, which is triple of Genoa-Savona.

For non-experts, the interest China has in owning ports as "physical places" is not immediately understandable: docks, piers, cranes, warehouses for storing goods, yards for containers. I struggled to find logic in it. I reasoned by comparing a nation to a company. If I'm a smartphone manufacturer, and I want to export them all over the world, I don't even need to buy trucks or ships or planes to transport those products. Nor do I need to own a highway. The infrastructures are at everyone's service, when I need them I use them and pay a toll, stop. So, what need does China have to own the physical spaces where its ships and goods must arrive? The answer, indeed the answers, were given to me by the heads of the port of Genoa. First of all, if you are an owner and own ships, controlling the port means that your cargo will have priority and those of others may have to wait at anchor, burdened with higher costs. Then there's an invisible benefit. If the Chinese giant Cosco owns an Italian port – they explained to me – it transforms it into a «cost centre». In its complex transnational accounting, the shipping and logistics giant makes Genoa a burden, a negative element of its operations; the profits he "boards" to the ship and takes them all to China. Even the taxes on those profits end up in Beijing. For the octopus of the Silk Roads, the maritime corridors also become channels for the transfer of wealth, like a gigantic vacuum cleaner that sucks the proceeds of the business towards the center of the empire.

American multinationals have long learned these tricks, see the immense tax avoidance of big digital companies such as Amazon, Apple and Google. Chinese multinationals are no different. A drain on profits and tax revenues is one of the streams set to course through the veins of the Belt and Road. Added to this is the strategic issue. That is, the specter of the real cold war, the embargo scenarios. This is easy to understand even for a non-navigation logistics expert. China has enjoyed the objective protection of the United States for at least thirty years. It is thanks to the global gendarme of the US Navy - paid for by the American taxpayer - that the shipping lanes are safe. This security was important for China: without having to shoulder the same military burden as the United States, it was able to send its merchant ships to invade the planet with products made in China, so much did it know that those cargo ships would not be attacked by pirates (if not rarely) nor by hostile foreign powers. The American empire has protected all global trade, we have all been a bit parasitic in enjoying the order that reigned over the seas thanks to Uncle Sam. Now, however, China sees a different chapter in history unfolding. It cannot exclude that America disengages from its role as guarantor of the capitalist order. That system of shared rules that was codified in the World Trade Organization is close to the Americans and not just because Donald Trump says so. So even on the question of routes and access to ports, Beijing wants to protect itself: owning piers and docks protects against reprisals in the uncertain future to come.

The dilemmas that Italy has to deal with concern all of Europe. If we Italians are grappling with the Chinese advance in our ports, the United Kingdom has had a taste of a similar challenge in the richest of its infrastructures: the London Stock Exchange, which also owns that of Milan. It happened on September 11, 2019, with a really curious choice of calendar. Eighteen years earlier al-Qaeda, with the attack on the Twin Towers, had struck a fatal blow against a symbol of American capitalism: Wall Street and therefore the New York Stock Exchange are just a few steps away from the World Trade Center. On 11 September 2019, a bloodless, painless, but no less symbolic offensive began towards another global financial center. That day the former colony attempted to buy the capital of the empire that had owned it. Hong Kong Exchanges and Clearing, the government company that owns the Hong Kong Stock Exchange, has launched a 32 billion pound hostile takeover bid on the London Stock Exchange. The date was significant and surprising for other reasons as well. The UK was in the midst of the Brexit storm; the city of Hong Kong was in the throes of popular protests. The takeover bid was rejected by the British and that first approach yielded no results. «Stock exchanges are institutions linked to the nation-state, they are civic assets, this is an obstacle to transnational acquisitions» commented the «Financial Times» on the day of the takeover bid. In reality, this has not prevented the creation of supranational mega-exchanges, as demonstrated by the passage of the Milan Stock Exchange under the control of the British one. However, sovereignty issues in the past hindered the takeover that the Germans of Deutsche Börse Ag had launched on the London Stock Exchange. Much more sensational would have been if the former Chinese colony of His British Majesty had managed to buy what historically had been its mother house.

The mere fact that the Hong Kong Stock Exchange was able to imagine, plan and engineer a takeover bid for London says a lot about the reversal of the balance of power between «us and them». The strategy of the New Silk Roads concerns infrastructures of all types and categories, tangible and intangible, physical and virtual. Finance is a strategic infrastructure, and is one of the few sectors where the UK still has a global role. It is also a key sector in Brexit scenarios. Proponents of Britain's divorce from the European Union have envisioned a Singapore-style future for their island. That is, the idea that the United Kingdom (or what will be left of it, assuming that Scotland and Northern Ireland want to stay there) can thrive alone in the midst of many giants, such as Singapore which is between China and India. That "Singapore-like" future, for the British, would involve a role as a tax haven and offshore financial center. This does not preclude their stock exchange from ending up in Chinese hands one day, however... And the detail does not escape notice that while the Western stock exchanges are almost all privatised, Hong Kong's is controlled by the local government, in turn dominated by that of Beijing.

One could argue that *business is business* or, in the Latin version, *pecunia non olet*. Money has no smell even if it's renminbi (or yuan) or, in this case, Hong Kong dollars. If Chinese companies make acquisitions in Europe, as American multinationals have done for a century now, what's wrong with that? As long as they act in a capitalist logic, Chinese money invested in our companies can enrich us all, improve efficiency, create jobs. Or not? One must be aware of the political price, to respond. A concrete example of the consequences is offered by those small European countries which were among the first "co-opted" within the Belt and Road. Portugal, Greece and Hungary are - in proportion to their GDP - among the major recipients of Chinese investments in infrastructure. Coincidentally, their governments have repeatedly blocked the European Union when it tries to criticize China for human rights abuses, in Tibet or against the Uyghurs. Lisbon and several Balkan capitals have also opposed the idea of introducing controls on Chinese investments in strategic sectors such as advanced technologies and telecoms. A senior official of the European Commission, under anonymity, made this disturbing confession: "We are now in the situation where China essentially has veto power within the EU institutions" (quoted by Julianne Smith and Torrey Taussig, The Old *World and the Middle Kingdom* , in «Foreign Affairs», September-October 2019). Chinese investments have already had a side effect, effectively reducing the sovereignty of the receiving countries.

The most interesting case in Europe is that of Germany. The richest and most powerful nation in the Union has suddenly moved from the ranks of pro-Chinese to those of anti-Chinese, to use a simple label. The conversion was spectacular and it is important to reconstruct its dynamics. In the last thirty years, Germany had perhaps been the most pro-Chinese nation in Europe, regardless of whether the chancellor was a Social Democrat or a Christian Democrat. We understand why: Germany is the only major European economy to have almost always had a trade surplus with China. Really nice exploit. The Chinese have been in love with German technology for decades: they adore Mercedes, Audi, BMW, power plants and industrial machinery made in Germany. Today as many as 5,200 German companies are based in China, where they employ over one million people. 40 percent of the cars produced by the Volkswagen group are sold on the market of the People's Republic.

With such satisfactory results, Germany had no reason to criticize the Chinese. Indeed, he implicitly supported them, in the face of criticism from America. I remember, at the time of Barack Obama, the unmentionable Berlin-Beijing axis. The two "mercantilist" nations, with the highest commercial assets on the planet, against the nation in perennial deficit. Obama contested (rightly) the parasitic effect of their behavior. Nations that accumulate macroscopic commercial assets are driven by the consumption of others and therefore enrich themselves by holding back the growth of others. China and Germany are two very different economies, but there is this affinity: they consider the rest of the world a market that must always remain open, but they don't care as much about the others. Again in 2013, proving how solid the Berlin-Beijing axis was, Angela Merkel blocked a European proposal to impose punitive duties on solar panels made in China. Those panels were exported to Europe in clear *dumping* , i.e. sold at prices lower than the cost of production, thanks to Chinese public subsidies. It is a form of unfair competition, expressly prohibited by WTO rules. But Merkel prevented that behavior harmful to European companies from being sanctioned, in the name of her excellent relations with Xi Jinping.

The Germans closed their eyes for a long time, even when it was clear that the Chinese were also stealing a lot of industrial secrets from them. I remember an episode that dates back to the years in which I was following the US-China negotiations on joining the WTO from California and was preparing my move to Beijing. Landing from the San Francisco-Shanghai flight at the turn of the millennium, I noticed the unusual form of transport made in Germany waiting for us passengers at the airport. A magnificent high-speed train, whose only function was to take us from the terminal to the city, a stretch of a few tens of kilometers along which the convoy did not even have time to reach cruising speed. And it didn't take us all the way to the center of Shanghai. No, the bullet train picked us up at the airport and left us in Pudong, the business district full of skyscrapers, the first Chinese Manhattan. But not all passengers were bound for Pudong, so if your destination was central Shanghai you'd have to transfer to a taxi. Uncomfortable. Last anomaly, the train interrupted the service very early in the evening, penalizing the passengers of numerous flights.

Like all passing foreigners, I asked the Chinese why there were so many inconsistencies. Their government had bought from Siemens a train made to hurtle at 300 per hour over straights of many hundreds of kilometres, which, for example, would have been perfect for connecting Shanghai to Beijing. Instead, he used it on such a short journey that a subway would have been enough. It's like buying a Ferrari and then only driving it up the exit ramp from the garage. The Chinese we asked these questions were evasive. Didn't they know, or did they pretend not to know? As for Siemens and the German government which had supported them in the battle to win that order, they were confident: you will see – they said – that this first section is only serving as a test. When the Chinese authorities are convinced that the technology made in Germany is also the best for high-speed railways, they will open up an immense market for connections over great distances.

The Germans were deluding themselves. For years the train continued to shuttle. Then the People's Republic really took the leap to high-speed lines. They built thousands of kilometers of it, the largest network in the world. From Beijing to Shanghai, from Shanghai to Hangzhou, further south to Guangzhou, the entire industrialized coastal strip was connected; later construction towards the interior regions also began. Now all over China you see convoys speeding by at 300 an hour. What about German technology? There's no need. High-speed trains are 100 percent made in China. Even if they look like drops of water to the German ones. That's what the Siemens "toy" was for. The Chinese government had bought the Ferrari and kept it almost stationary in the garage, not out of inefficiency, but to take it apart and put it back together, piece by piece. «Reverse engineering», this procedure is defined: a classic of industrial espionage. The Germans, therefore, were already duped twenty years ago. Yet they limited themselves to mild protests, because overall their business was doing well in China.

There has been a revival, but it's much more recent. The straw that broke the camel's back was the "Made in China 2025" plan. Wanted by Xi Jinping, it illustrates the systematic strategy with which the Beijing government aims to achieve world supremacy in many strategic technologies: robotics and artificial intelligence, renewable energies and electric cars, aerospace, telecoms and many other sectors. That plan looks a lot like a similar German program called "Industry 4.0." But Germany is bound by European rules that prohibit state aid, or monopolistic mergers. China does not have these limitations, it feeds its "national champions" with subsidies and public aid. When Xi announced the "Made in China 2025" project, big German industry opened its eyes and realized that it was among the predestined victims of that plan. Between now and 2025, i.e. very quickly, Beijing aims to systematically replace the German technologies it imported with as many domestic technologies. In short, the case of the Siemens train will be extended to all sectors: China will do it itself, rather than importing expensive Germanic know-how.

At this point the implicit pact linking German and Chinese interests is in crisis. An espionage scandal was added in 2017. Berlin's secret services have accused China of having created 10,000 false identities on the LinkedIn social network, with the aim of spying on German citizens, especially ministers, parliamentarians, senior public administration executives. The revelation recalled an incident involving Barack Obama: on the occasion of his official visit to Berlin, WikiLeaks had revealed that US intelligence had even put Merkel's cell phone under surveillance. While it's not news that secret services are also spying on allied nations, the scoop poisoned Obama's visit. But the reaction was different in the two cases. While Obama officially apologized to the chancellor, the Chinese deny all wrongdoing and therefore feel no need to apologise. Furthermore, in the United States the independent press severely criticized the spying on Merkel. In China, however, the media do not report negative news about their government.

In any case, it must arrive at the beginning of 2019 for a reversal in Germany's strategy to occur. In January of this year, the German Confindustria published a very harsh report against the "Made in China 2025" plan and urged member companies to reduce their dependence on the Chinese market. In the same period, Merkel's pressure is decisive in pushing the European Commission to review its entire approach to China. For the first time in history, the People's Republic is defined as "a strategic rival" in the official position of Brussels. In fact, the definition follows that of the United States. It's a breakthrough. While strongly denouncing Donald Trump's tariffs, the European authorities agree with him on a fundamental point: China has become a threat. This also explains the harshness of Brussels, Berlin and Paris towards the Conte I government, on the occasion of the signing of the Memorandum on the Belt and Road. To the Italians, those criticisms appeared hypocritical, since they came from countries that had received much more Chinese capital than us. Very true. However, the Xi-Conte operation caused a sensation due to the wrong timing: Italy's entry into the New Silk Roads took place just when the European Union had revised its approach to China in a negative sense.

Does German repentance, course correction, mean that Europe will be forced to align with the United States in the new Cold War? This is not safe at all. European and American interests do not coincide. Belonging to the club of liberal democracies, the common values of the West do not necessarily force us to march together. Switzerland and Finland are Western liberal democracies, they share our principles, but remain neutral and do not participate in alliances such as NATO. There is a real temptation for Europe: that of carving out for itself a role of "third force", halfway between the United States and China, also obtaining advantages from it. After all, this also happened during the First Cold War. For example, the US-USSR tension did not prevent the social democratic chancellor Willy Brandt from pursuing an "Eastern policy" which opened up some markets in the Soviet bloc to German industry; Italy, from Enrico Mattei to Giulio Andreotti, pursued a pro-Arab policy in the Mediterranean which distanced itself from the United States. Our autonomy, however, was modest. We knew that the Soviet Union had not hesitated to use military force to assert limited sovereignty in its sphere of influence: with tanks in Budapest in 1956, in Prague in 1968. We knew that Moscow's nuclear missiles were aimed at our. The protective umbrella of the United States was the glue of the Atlantic alliance. Beyond certain limits we could not distinguish ourselves from the Washington line.

Today the situation is not as clear as it was during the First Cold War. Unlike the USSR, China poses no immediate military threat to us: it has no troops or missiles on our borders. His invasion seems exquisitely economic, you may like it or not but it does not involve bloodshed. And we need its capital. But we are dependent on the United States for other forms of security. For example, Europe has no integrated intelligence services; nor a common defense against cyber-attacks. In the new digital wars, asymmetric and waged with potentially blinding weapons against our most crucial infrastructures, we Europeans are clueless. We have pursued the dream of building a "herbivorous power": that is, a new type of post-modern force, capable of radiating international influence not with weapons but through its economic, scientific, educational wealth, and the quality of its rights . But when a phase of international tensions reopens, and we are surrounded by carnivorous powers armed to the teeth, what is left for us to do? Both the United States and China have a "holistic" geopolitical approach, for them economic interests and military strategies are one. Donald Trump glibly threatens to withdraw his military support for allies if they do not align with US demands on foreign trade. Xi Jinping uses the weight of his foreign investments to blackmail other governments on Taiwan, Hong Kong, Tibet. Will we Europeans, who usually distinguish trade negotiations from foreign or military policy choices, end up crushed by the reborn bipolar logic?

I return to the place from which I started, Genoa. Among the data that the local authorities have provided me, here are some that make you think. If we exclude oil and intra-EU trade, Chinese goods represent 22 percent of goods arriving in Italy by sea. For their part, the United States is the first destination for goods departing by sea. The dilemma is clear. The particular observatory that is the port of Genoa (through which 65 percent of Lombardy's extra-EU trade passes, 80 percent of Piedmont's) gives us a snapshot of a more general problem. Italian, European. We are in a situation of almost equal, specular and symmetrical dependence on the two superpowers. One, America, is an indispensable outlet market as well as a historic ally. The other, China, has become an equally essential supplier and invests heavily in our country. It was a harmless situation in the thirty years of peaceful globalization. It can become a trap now that the tide has changed.

However, a chapter on the Chinese in Italy cannot be limited to talking about grand imperial strategies, penetration into our strategic infrastructures, or into advanced technologies. As in other parts of the world, here too there is a Chinese reality which is made up of entrepreneurs looking for opportunities, autonomous subjects, which we must not confuse with the Beijing government's plans for conquest. We have become accustomed to seeing among us the very small entrepreneurs of the diaspora, the emigrated merchants, the famous Chinese of via Paolo Sarpi (Milan), piazza Vittorio (Rome), or of the textile district of Prato: those who buy businesses with briefcases of black money, or exploit clandestine labor under the stairs. These are well-known stories that I too wrote about in my explorations of Italian and world Chinatowns. Obviously this wild micro-capitalism of the diaspora, in the wild, is a spontaneous dust that is independent of Xi Jinping's strategies. In some cases it dates back to the 19th century. He knows how to use his own networks of *guanxi* , a term that evokes the English *networking* , but which for us can allude to mafia methods.

Then there is another export capitalism, very recent and of a very different caliber. In Italy in particular, a new Chinese entrepreneurship is emerging which is attracted by a love story. The fascination that our country exerts on the Chinese is an important factor. The myth of Italy – I know something about it as an expatriate for life – is a very strong phenomenon in every corner of the planet. Americans and English, Germans and French, Brazilians and Indians adore the beauties of our country, from the landscape to the archaeological heritage, from ancient Rome to the Renaissance, plus our lifestyle and the many wonders of Made in Italy. For the Chinese, a mixture of astonishment and envy is added to all this. They belong to a civilization older than ours but whose vestiges have been little and badly preserved. They are enraptured by all the ancient that is still clearly visible in Pompeii or in the Imperial Forums, in our medieval villages or in our seventeenth-century squares; they see a sort of ideal thread that reunites Leonardo, Michelangelo, Raphael, Bramante, Palladio and Brunelleschi with the creativity of contemporary Italian design.

Over the course of a decade, this falling in love has accompanied a transformation in the typology of Chinese visitors. At first, Venice and Florence were invaded by masses of Chinese - let's face it - rude and vulgar, ignorant and cumbersome. That group tourism still exists and will continue to grow. But there is a new phenomenon, that of the cultured and refined Chinese, who travel as a couple or in small groups of friends, go on an exploration of less obvious regions and places, choose farmhouses or secluded inns. Luxury tourism in search of a truer and more coveted Italy, for them a precious object of desire.

This also happens in the business world. There are Chinese capitalists whose investments are guided by a kind of aesthetic philosophy. It is my encounter with one of these that I want to tell you about, because it is another facet of the Chinese advance, different from Huawei or port investments.

The entrepreneur in question was born in New York but is one hundred percent Chinese. He loves Italy and has made it the preferred destination for his investments, but he would never dream of buying a football team. When I meet her in April 2018, she is 38 years old. Heir to one of the largest capitalist families in the Far East, he feels an obvious annoyance with the world of so-called luxury. He doesn't say it, out of innate courtesy, but it is clear that he considers it populated by peasants, especially on the customer side. He calls himself Stephen Cheng, anglicizing and inverting the traditional order between first and last name, as many Chinese who have international businesses do, to make life easier for us Westerners. His story may appear disconcerting, or perhaps quite normal. It serves to sweep away stereotypes and prejudices about the Chinese entrepreneurial class, and to understand one of its possible lines of evolution. (I found traces of it in the aforementioned film *Crazy Rich Asians* , even though that fiction is set in Singapore.)

To begin with, like many grandsons of big business leaders, Cheng wanted to do anything but continue the family business. His grandfather, he explains to me when I meet him in his Milanese office in via dei Bossi (behind La Scala), «created the largest naval transport company in Hong Kong», but he studied at Harvard «history of cinema and photography, because my true passion has always been art». In his Hong Kong he opened «the first and most important gallery of experimental visual art, an all-black place inside, where arts, music and multimedia installations intersect». The family has always tried to bring him back to the fold, towards the business world: in 2005 they convinced him to work for three years at the American bank Goldman Sachs, then they almost pushed his future wife, Helen Wang, a multi-graduate in business, into his arms and finance. The two jointly manage the family office that diversifies the group's investments, The World Wide Investment Co., based in Hong Kong. But the jewel to which they devote the most loving care is Nuo Capital, the Italian rib. It is here that Cheng manages to combine investment with his passion for art.

Between a flight to New York for an exhibition at the Park Avenue Armory, and a stop in Berlin where he owns an avant-garde music vinyl record production company, Stephen and Helen stop in Milan once every two months . When I meet them in 2018 it is during the Salone del Mobile or Design Week: high quality Italian furniture is one of the sectors where they are already active. Cheng summarizes his investment philosophy for me: «First, we want to be minority shareholders, to accompany entrepreneurs in whom we have the utmost confidence. Second, we invest for the long term. Thirdly, we want to guide Italian excellence towards Asia». He sees a positive role in both directions: his network of Chinese acquaintances can open up that market to small-medium sized Italian companies, which alone would not make it. But focusing on very high quality is also for him "a way to raise the standards of the Chinese, both consumers and producers".

Among the examples of companies in which he has already invested, in the furniture sector of excellence, Cheng cites «the Promemoria of the designer Romeo Sozzi (Como), and the Bottega Ghianda, a cabinet-making art that has been manufacturing objects in Valmadrera (Lecco) for two centuries of wood without the use of nails". Then there is the Artemest digital platform, designed to promote Italian craftsmanship and open up global markets for it. It helps that in Asia the Cheng family's business includes the development of luxury hotels, a natural market outlet for Italian furnishings of that level. In a different sector there is the partnership with Vittorio Moretti of Bellavista wine (Franciacorta). According to Cheng, "Chinese and Italians have many values in common, among these the culture of the family as the basis of the company, and the ability to transfer the same creativity of great artists into the world of production". Today's China in the West is still identified as a Moloch of mass production, "but in our DNA there is the furniture of the Ming dynasty, very refined, and this makes us receptive to Italian beauty". Not all prejudices about the Chinese are unfounded, Cheng knows. He is the first to object to certain tycoons of his compatriots "who invest in the West because they want to bring capital out of China, diversify their portfolio in terms of currencies and risk". I will not repeat, in order not to disturb entire fan groups, your thoughts on who invests in football teams...

Cheng thinks he is just a precursor, the vanguard of an evolution that will soon involve many others: «I see it all around me, in Hong Kong or Shanghai and Beijing: in my generation there are those who are already overcoming the phase of nouveau riche, brazen ostentation, opulent consumption for its own sake, without an idea of sustainability. It takes time to develop a new type of taste and sensitivity, but then the change happens very quickly, especially among young people». It may be a coincidence, but this philosophy fits into a favorable political context: ever since Xi Jinping unleashed his campaigns against corruption - slapping many hundreds of communist leaders in jail - being seen in a Lamborghini on the streets of Beijing or with too many Hermès and Louis Vuitton accessories can become risky.

And in any case Cheng does not want to appear a snob: «Excellence alone is not enough, I want to be able to connect these Italian jewels with the megatrends of online commerce and digital consumption». The name Nuo, the young spouses explain to me, is the acronym of New Understanding Opportunities, but in Mandarin it also means "promise". For them, the promise is to remain faithful to an Italian idea of sober elegance, which has seduced them.

Cheng's story is somewhat exceptional, not representative of the entire Chinese economy. Not surprisingly, the young entrepreneur comes from a Hong Kong family. The Chinese island has absorbed and reworked the British colonial influence; despite having returned to the motherland, it continues to distinguish itself from the People's Republic, including in political protests. At the same time this story is typical of a rapidly evolving Chinese world, with a fast learning curve, capable of throwing us off guard. We cannot enclose it in a few stereotypes, because they immediately turn out to be outdated.

.

VII

Finance, myths and legends

———

It's an old refrain: if you owe your bank a million, you're in trouble, but if you owe them a billion, your bank is in trouble. If the debtor is America, and its banker is China, the rule applies more than ever.

Among my European interlocutors - and also among some Americans - I often encounter the idea that in the new cold war it is Beijing that has the final weapon, the superbomb that can crash the adversary: the American debt. "After all," I hear people who consider themselves well-informed say, "it is China that holds the majority of US Treasuries. If he threatens not to buy them again, America is on its knees, it goes bankrupt." This urban legend is as widespread as it is fallacious. First of all, it is blatantly factually inaccurate. Furthermore, those who believe in this fable do not understand some fundamental rules of economics.

Starting with the facts: it is not true that China is the first creditor of the United States. The metaphor of the bank is funny but it needs to be brought back to reality. Statistics on US Treasury funding are public, accurate, up-to-date and transparent. First in financing their federal debt are Americans themselves, beginning with the various branches of their Social Security, then through the Federal Reserve, i.e. the central bank. It is these national entities that have by far the primacy among the purchasers of Treasury Bonds and T-Bills (behind these terms there are securities similar to BOTs and BTPs, but issued in Washington).

If we look only at foreign buyers, China has recently been overtaken by Japan, so in the list of "bankers" it ranks fourth. Over the years, the Chinese arsenal has decreased because Beijing's commercial surplus with the rest of the world, which is the primary source of foreign exchange reserves, has decreased. According to the latest data for 2019, US Treasury bonds held by China were 1,112 billion dollars against 1,122 for Japan. These are considerable figures, no doubt, but they must be seen in the right proportion. The total of American public debt outstanding in the form of securities reached 22,000 billion in 2019. China therefore owns just over 5 percent of it. Even if he decides – in an irrational and self-destructive kamikaze gesture, as I will explain – to sell all those bonds in one fell swoop to "hurt America", what would happen? A projected sale of 1.5 trillion Treasury bills (more than China has) measured that it would raise US interest rates by 0.5 percent. Certainly not an Apocalypse. Moreover, every year the Federal Reserve itself sells hundreds of billions of bonds on the market, a mountain of public securities that it had bought at the time of *quantitative easing* to counter the recession. It would be enough for the Fed to suspend those sales to mitigate the impact of "Chinese sabotage".

The idea that America depends on only one creditor is pure fantasy. But even more bizarre is the idea that Beijing could stop buying US Treasuries any day now. First of all, a country that has been accumulating trade surpluses for decades, therefore seeing dollars, euros, pounds, yen flowing into its homeland, needs to manage its currency reserves carefully. For about seventy-five years there has been no safer and more liquid investment than the dollar, and of all dollar investments, government bonds are the strongest. Of course, even German bonds, the Bunds, are safe: but there are few of them on the market because Germany has a surplus balance sheet; moreover, since 2019 Bunds have been giving negative yields. The Chinese central bank would harm itself, mismanage its assets, harm the interests of its government and its citizens if it suddenly launched a boycott of the US Treasury.

Another even more pressing pressure works on China: a large exporting nation needs buyers for its products; stop giving credit to those who buy his goods, impoverish his own customer, is the last thing a good merchant would do. *Dulcis in fundo* : the disaffection of the Chinese from the dollar would cause the American currency to fall, therefore it would make Chinese exports more expensive, and would damage precisely the made in China. It would be pure self-defeat to sink the dollar.

In fact Beijing, when it is in difficulty, tends to do the exact opposite, that is, it buys even more dollars to weaken its currency and boost exports. And we must remember an asymmetry that makes the People's Republic structurally more fragile: as long as it maintains controls on capital movements, restrictions on the export of currency, the communist nomenklatura reveals that it does not want to submit to the judgment of the markets because it knows that its citizens they could put their savings elsewhere, from Tokyo to Singapore, from London to New York, to Zurich, "voting with the money" to express their disagreement with one or another government policy. For all these reasons, the urban legend about the famous "fatal weapon" makes no sense.

However, however... If that legend has taken deep roots in the Western imagination, one of the reasons is that the Chinese have always tried to give credence to it. Even more so when, in the great crisis of 2008-2009, they felt betrayed by America and feared that their export-driven development model would crash. It's a story I remember well. I followed her day by day, shuttling between the two sides of the Pacific: 2009 was the year in which I concluded my Chinese life, and organized my return to the United States. With one eye I followed then-President Hu Jintao, with the other, Barack Obama. Reconstructing the "roller coaster" of that period, the spasms and contortions of the economy and the markets, serves to evaluate the evolution of the balance of power between America and China in the field of finance. Because one thing is certain: the financial markets will be one of the terrains where the new cold war will take place; the world of stock exchanges and currencies, capital flows will be influenced by the next stages of the challenge between the two superpowers. Reconstructing the background of the last ten years also helps to understand that the clash has been maturing for some time and is not only linked to Trump.

January 2009. Destined to become the American president most disliked by Chinese leaders (much more than Trump), Barack Obama took office in the White House only a few days ago. His administration begins by attacking China. It was precisely in those days that the question circulated on the markets: what would happen if Beijing reacted by stopping financing the American public debt? The specter of a fracture in the Sino-American financial bond – «Chimerica» – peeps out on the most liquid market on the planet, the one where Treasury bills issued in Washington are exchanged. The risks of a US-China trade tension are shaking for a few days the thirty-year Treasury

Bonds, one of the safest securities and traditionally a safe haven for investors. Thirty-year T-Bonds sold off as soon as the US Senate released the text of the hearing of new Treasury Secretary Tim Geithner appointed by Obama. There is the accusation against China of «manipulating its own currency». It's a strong accusation, one that no Bush administration Treasury secretary has ever wanted to make openly. It can pave the way for commercial retaliation against Made in China.

What scared the markets is the rumor that in a protectionist escalation Beijing could use the financial weapon, reducing its purchases of US Treasury bills. The last twenty years of growth in the world economy has been based on the complementarity between the United States and the People's Republic: the high debt of American consumers was matched by the high savings of Chinese families; the US trade deficits that swelled Beijing's foreign exchange reserves were regularly "laundered" by the Chinese central bankers with the subscription of American public bonds. In turn, China had a clear advantage. By giving credit to the United States, it fueled demand for its exports. That system partially jammed in the months of 2008-2009 which saw the handover between George W. Bush and his democratic successor: the recession is the physiological and brutal way in which the American economy reduces consumption, imports and household debts. But the reduction of private debt is accompanied by a boom in public debt, the higher the larger the state investment maneuver launched by Obama to counter the recession.

Washington will continue to need foreign lenders for its soaring federal debt for many years. And it is not only China's possible reaction that is frightening, but the very dimension of American government needs. As a result of the bailout plans for the banks (700 billion dollars) and to relaunch growth (825 billion), also taking into account maturing securities and a deficit that already exceeds 8 per cent of GDP (later it will arrive to 12 per cent), in 2009 the US Treasury must issue at least 2 trillion new T-bonds. Such a large inflow can be a severe test for the appetite of investors, who until now in the "risk-flight" phases had voraciously absorbed Treasuries by driving their yields down (below zero for shorter maturities).

What could have induced Geithner to risk a tussle with the Chinese creditor? The new Treasury secretary is no fool: he has already worked as a senior official in that department under the Clinton administration, was at the International Monetary Fund, headed the Federal Reserve Bank of New York, the most important operating branch of the central bank. If Geithner thinks he can raise his voice with the Chinese at this stage, it is because a real crisis of no confidence in American T-bonds is not around the corner. The markets have no safer alternative, except for an illiquid investment like gold. In Europe, the banking crises, the deterioration of public finances and the downgrading of some Mediterranean countries have made investors more reluctant to buy Treasury bills in the Pigs area (Portugal, Italy, Greece, Spain). In Asia, too, the economy is deteriorating at an impressive speed, with Chinese growth almost halved (in the last quarter of 2008, the annual GDP had increased by 6.8 percent. The previous year, the annual increase had been 10 .6 per cent). In such a bleak picture, the dollar immediately returned to its status as a safe haven currency. The index that measures the value of the dollar against a basket of currencies (euro, yen, pound sterling, Swiss franc, Swedish krona, Canadian dollar) gained 18 percent from June 2008 to January 2009. Incredible but true: just as it is the toxic finance of Wall Street the trigger of the systemic crisis, it is there on Wall Street that savings from all over the world flow in search of salvation.

September 2011. The Chinese were called to the role of «white knight» in the United States, in the midst of the systemic disaster of 2008: the most important operation was the 1.2 billion dollar investment in the storm-hit Morgan Stanley bank ; another 650 million were placed by the Chinese in the Blackstone private equity fund; minor stakes in Citigroup and Bank of America. Furious controversies followed in China on the wisdom of those operations. At its worst, when the Dow Jones charts had plummeted to historic lows, Chinese managers were accused by their *constituency* of having burned domestic resources in a rash but futile bailout of American banks. Already three years after the balance of that operation is less negative.

The protagonists of this match are two financial giants. First there is the «parent company», the state body which manages the foreign exchange reserves of the central bank. These reserves, the result of years of commercial assets that China accumulates with the rest of the world, are the richest on the planet: in 2011 they reached 3.2 trillion dollars. The English acronym of this body (State Administration of Foreign Exchange) is Safe, as "safe" or even "safe", and is an effective synthesis of its investment philosophy. At the rate at which central bank reserves are being replenished by new commercial assets, the Safe had to invest $275 billion in the first half of 2011 alone. This means that, if it wanted to, the Safe could subscribe to all Italian public bonds maturing throughout the year. But it would be unsafe, precisely: it is no coincidence that the central bank continues to reinvest the majority of reserves in US government bonds. Despite the jitters aroused in Beijing by the downgrading that Standard & Poor's inflicted on the US Treasury, the market prices of long-term Treasury Bonds are holding up very well.

As for diversifying from the dollar towards other currencies, to remain « safe » the Beijing central bank favors German Bunds and Japanese debt securities. China's repeated announcements of massive bond purchases of Mediterranean countries have always turned out to be exaggerated. In July 2010, rumors of support for Spain had a short-lived impact on the markets (Safe bought 500 million 10-year bonds, a modest investment). In October of the same year, Premier Wen Jiabao paid a visit to Athens and even then the expectations of maxi bond purchases were short-lived. What was real was the entry of the Chinese logistics giant Cosco into the port management of Athens.

This is where the other, more aggressive dimension of Chinese strategy takes over. The protagonist in this case is the China Investment Corporation (CIC), Beijing's sovereign wealth fund. Its resources always come from the same source: the central bank's foreign exchange reserves. However, the CIC has more freedom of action and different functions: a spearhead for China's penetration into the global economy. Its statute attributes to it a « commercial orientation and purely economic-financial objectives ». The CIC is a company that must be accountable to its shareholders (the Beijing government) and present year-end dividends. However, this does not exclude that it could serve as a *long arm* for strategic objectives such as the acquisition of advanced technologies, managerial know-how, bridgeheads on promising markets or in activities where China has yet to acquire a competitive advantage. The CIC was born in 2007 with an initial endowment of 200 billion dollars, four years later it already manages a portfolio of acquisitions of over 410 billion. Its diversification towards corporate investments is evident in the United States, where the Chinese have entered as shareholders in Apple, Coca-Cola, Johnson & Johnson, Motorola, Visa. Geographically, direct investments remain focused on the United States with 42 percent, followed by Asia with 30 percent, while Europe only comes in third place with 22 percent.

However, Europe too has an example of diversification towards industrial activities: taking advantage of the 2008 crisis, the Chinese acquired control of Volvo from Ford. In America their ambitions are not always indulged. Twice Washington barred the door to Chinese investment under Bush and Obama: when they attempted to acquire a Californian oil company (Unocal) and when the telecom giant Huawei tried to buy 3Com, a company that also supplies military technologies to the Pentagon.

February 2014. America came out of the recession in record time: already in the summer of 2009. China has never even entered it. Thanks to a robust intervention by state capitalism, pushing investments in infrastructure and construction projects, the Beijing government has shown that it has studied John Maynard Keynes: in depressions it is up to the state to step forward. It was in that period, thanks to such an effective performance, that a superiority complex, the belief that one's own political system was better than the Western one, became increasingly strong in the upper levels of the communist nomenklatura. But at the beginning of 2014 it is China that is showing signs of financial fragility. The Americans are sounding the alarm: the detonator could be the competitive devaluation of the renminbi (or yuan), the Chinese currency. Its depreciation in February marks its heaviest fall since 2005. It is a sharp turnaround after years of slow rise of the Chinese currency.

The consequences are many, political and financial. In Washington, the chorus of protests against the Beijing government is growing, accused of not keeping to the agreements. And in a year of legislative elections, many US parliamentarians are calling for retaliatory tariff and customs measures to punish Made in China. *China intervenes to weaken the yuan* is a headline in the Wall Street Journal. The newspaper has no doubts: "It is the Chinese central bank that is pushing downwards". Among the political reactions from Washington is that of the Democratic group leader in the Senate, Charles Schumer: "China must allow the yuan to move freely based on market forces, even if the market pushes it upwards." In the House, a bill that would impose punitive tariffs on imports from China has garnered more than half of the necessary signatures. For now, the Obama administration is silent. Also because the United States is not entirely innocent in terms of competitive devaluations. Indeed, the "currency war", as the Brazilian Economy Minister Guido Mantega defined it two years earlier, was initiated by the Federal Reserve. The massive creation of liquidity that the US central bank has operated to revive growth has also had the weakening of the dollar as a side effect.

The American "manual" was subsequently studied and copied by other central banks: the last one was that of Japan, which also manipulated the currency downwards, allowing the weak yen to help exports made in Japan. Naturally, both Washington and Tokyo reject these comparisons. Neither the Fed nor the Bank of Japan "manipulate" their currencies directly, since exchange rates are set by supply and demand on global markets (the influence of central banks is indirect, it affects interest rates, the creation of liquidity, and on expectations). The case of China is different because the renminbi or yuan continues to be a partially liberalized currency, whose external value is still governed by the government. There are macroeconomic risks if China tries to "export" its problems, or to get out of a slowdown in growth by relaunching exports through competitive devaluation.

August 2015. The devaluation of the yuan, in response to the slowdown in Chinese growth, is the first real test of the "special relationship" that has been established for many years between China and the West. The premises were the thaw between Richard Nixon and Mao Zedong (1972), then the capitalist reforms of Deng Xiaoping in the 1980s, but the real key date is 2001, the year of Beijing's entry into the World Trade Organization which consecrated its role in the new international division of labour. Since then, albeit with recurring frictions, an objective convergence of interests has prevailed. The American market has always remained very open to Chinese products, in return Beijing has diligently reinvested its commercial assets in US Treasury securities. To the point that there was talk of an implicit G2, a directory of two to govern the world.

Even with the European Union the level of interdependence-interpenetration has increased, as demonstrated by the large Chinese investments in the Old Continent, including Italy. China has behaved as a "responsible shareholder", the occasional even serious tensions (human rights, Tibet, cyber-attacks, expansionist aims towards Japan and the Philippines) have never prevented it from obeying the business is business *rule* . Never, however, has a Chinese leadership had to face a threat as serious as the current one, to national well-being and therefore to political stability. Will he be able to stand up to them without destabilizing relations with the West? Will Beijing remain a "responsible shareholder"?

In the 1980s, major currency storms (in the dollar-DM-yen triangle) were managed within the G7, but they were all allied to each other and essentially vassals of Washington. Today global governance is weak, compared to what is at stake. In the immediate future, the problem that will arise is that of an "orderly" devaluation of the yuan. Because markets are notoriously prone to *overshooting* , and when they go down a road they tend to overshoot. Moderating excesses is in everyone's interest, but it requires a level of China-US-EU concertation that cannot be taken for granted. In the end, the net result of a devaluation is always this: the fall of the renminbi makes 1.3 billion Chinese nominally "poorer", whose purchasing power is reduced; it makes our exports more expensive in what had been a driving market for years; vice versa, it makes everything that China produces cheaper.

It is neither strange nor uncommon for a country to try to pass on its problems to its neighbours. The Federal Reserve, after the 2008 crisis, began to print money in unprecedented quantities: 4.5 trillion dollars. One of the beneficial effects of that maneuver (*quantitative easing*) was the competitive devaluation of the dollar. The euro shot past 1.50 against the dollar. The American recovery was aided by this. Six years late, Mario Draghi finally managed to imitate the Fed, and it was the ECB's turn: print money, buy bonds, weaken the euro. Now China does. It is difficult to excommunicate her for this. His machine falters, Chinese exports fell by 8 percent in 2015. After the devaluation of the renminbi, the Monetary Fund is postponing the entry of the Chinese currency among its reserve currencies. Almost 1 trillion dollars of capital has left emerging countries over the past thirteen months. They are three sides of the same problem: the major global economic tensions today revolve around the difficulties of the Chinese dragon. No one can ignore this shock, everyone must incorporate the unknown factor of the People's Republic into their scenarios. Not that it is easy to get a reliable estimate: the same data on Chinese GDP are questioned by many experts. The current growth of 7 percent, although much lower than the average of the last two decades, is considered unreliable in the light of the heavy drop in import-export. Some speak of real growth that would be only half of the official figure. The IMF decision refers to the entry of the renminbi or yuan into the basket of currencies that form the "special drawing rights" of the supranational institution based in Washington. For now, only the dollar, euro, pound sterling and Japanese yen are listed.

Beijing aims to "promote" its currency, a significant step forward to strengthen China's global role. For the IMF, however, the renminbi is not yet a currency like the others, its value continues to be controlled by the government through numerous restrictions on the circulation of capital. Therefore, the entry of the renminbi into the IMF "basket" will be discussed again in a few months.

The Chinese evil is already infecting large areas of the world economy. The entire commodity sector is in the throes of a deflationary cycle, with oil and copper falling sharply: weakening Chinese demand is causing knock-on effects. Capital flight is triggering devaluations in countries as diverse as Australia and Indonesia, Singapore and Vietnam. Brazil is now close to undergoing a new rating downgrade, its government bonds risk becoming *junk-bonds* . No one is saved, among those economies that had benefited from the driving force of Chinese demand. The specter of sovereign defaults is reappearing on the horizon, especially as the currency reserves accumulated by emerging countries are dwindling visibly. As for the stock exchanges, no one is reassured by the fact that Beijing is entering "straight leg" into trading on the stock market, to stem the falls in stocks. Many companies listed on the Shanghai Stock Exchange have revealed that recently some public entities have entered their shareholding, raking up stocks on the market to curb their fall. It is a cordon sanitaire organized by the central government, a coalition of state-owned companies which stock market operators call "the national team".

January 2016. I close the Stock Exchange, so it stops falling. Indeed no, I reopen it. The disorientation of the Chinese government in the face of the crash is as frightening as the problems of the real economy that form the background. The show offered by the Beijing authorities during our Epiphany is disconcerting. Cornered by capital flight from the Shanghai stock market, the government reacted in an uncertain, contradictory way. In just forty-eight hours, the government did everything and the opposite of everything. It used administrative means, edicts from above, to counter the collapse by forcing public banks to buy bonds. He has launched ominous proclamations against the bearish speculators. He generously used *circuit breakers* , an expression borrowed from electrical systems: «spezzacircuito» in English, in Italian they are life-saving devices that prevent you from dying of electrocution. On the Stock Exchange, these are mechanisms for automatic interruption of exchanges, should price fluctuations exceed a certain threshold. Circuit *breakers* exist on many Western stock exchanges including Wall Street. But the Chinese authorities have made very abundant use of it. Up to deciding the total closure of the Stock Exchange, when it dropped too much. Finally the rethink. With an about-face, the authorities announced that the stock exchange would operate normally, without suspensions. The push-and-pull didn't reassure anyone.

This was superimposed by the effect of the devaluation. Even on the national currency, the yuan or renminbi, the Beijing government is playing with fire. It started devaluing it in August 2015, presenting its decision as an approximation to market values. The Chinese authorities, starting with the central bank, have repeatedly explained their intention to transform the renminbi into a fully convertible currency, which would entail the dismantling of restrictions on capital movements. The decision was welcomed by the International Monetary Fund, which in fact rewarded China in November 2015 by inserting the renminbi into its official currencies together with the dollar, euro, yen and pound. But this has raised investors' suspicions that President Xi Jinping also wants to help the export industry with a weak renminbi. The spiral of expectations has started: investors are now expecting the Chinese currency to go lower. And so they prefer to exit the Shanghai Stock Exchange in order not to suffer losses on securities denominated in a declining currency. Even Chinese savers consider it urgent to take shelter.

How do you explain the many mistakes made in those months by Xi Jinping and by the various authorities responsible for governing the economy, including the central bank, which is not independent of political power? One explanation involves the learning curve. Chinese leaders have shown competence and effectiveness in other fields of economic development, but global finance is still a new world for them. Furthermore, this ruling class has experienced thirty years of boom, now it has to deal with the first real crisis since China has been a global giant. It has had only two episodes of "near-crisis": the Sars epidemic of 2003, when the Chinese economy feared isolation (it lasted a few months); then the Great American Contraction of 2008-2009 which had heavy repercussions on Chinese exports. Faced with the current slowdown of 2015-2016, Xi Jinping would prefer not to reuse the public spending therapy that has burdened the economic system with too many debts, useless works, cathedrals in the desert, inefficiencies and corruption. Try to react to this crisis with new therapies. His "training" takes place in flight, in the midst of serious turbulence. Then there is the problem of consent, which even an authoritarian regime must address. Hundreds of millions of Chinese have invested their savings in the stock market. This China is embarking on a delicate transition, towards a horizon that could be summarized as follows: growing less but growing better. Before we get there, however, it can run into severe storms.

August 6, 2019. Flash forward three years and we are in the Trump era. The trade war is enriched by a new chapter. The general rehearsal of a parallel war, that of currencies, has begun between Washington and Beijing. It all started with the move by the Chinese central bank which caused the dollar-renminbi parity to slip below the symbolic level of 7 to 1 for the first time, which had not been crossed for years. The weakening of the renminbi-yuan is a move with which Xi can try to offset the effect of US tariffs. US customs duties automatically increase the price of Made in China, competitive devaluation has the opposite effect. Washington's reaction arrives: for the first time since 1994, and therefore for the first time since China integrated itself into the global economy, the US Treasury officially denounces it as a nation that "manipulates the currency", paving the way in theory to new sanctions. It is the formal declaration of a currency war that can prolong and amplify the tariff war. It is an additional piece in a legal arsenal that legitimizes future American retaliation.

The imbalance in trade between the two countries continues to be enormous: the US bilateral deficit was 167 billion dollars in the first half of this year. However, it is declining, in this sense the duties are working: American imports from China have decreased by 12 percent. Xi Jinping has less room for maneuver than his counterpart: since Beijing imports a fifth of what it exports to America, its ability to retaliate step by step with tariffs is already running out. An alternative is to offset US tariffs by making Chinese goods cheaper through devaluation. The war of coins had so far been avoided, because it has contraindications. China is also a major importer of raw materials, primarily oil, which pays in dollars. If the renminbi depreciates, its energy bill will automatically go up.

Another risk is capital flight. Chinese savers, fearful of the devaluation of their currency, may try to diversify their portfolios by increasing foreign securities. Exporting capital from China isn't as easy as from a Western country, but there are ways around currency restrictions, and both Chinese savers and businesses have resorted to them in times of fear in the past. This ties in with the US Treasury's complaint about currency manipulation. A premise of that denunciation is that the renminbi is effectively manipulable, ie controlled by the central bank and therefore by the Beijing government (the monetary authority in China is not independent of the executive). In reality, the Chinese currency navigates a hybrid system. It partly responds to market forces, supply and demand, such as the dollar or the euro, the Japanese yen or the British pound. In part, it is the People's Bank of China (Pboc, official name of the central bank) that directs its fluctuations. This hybrid model also results in the existence of two foreign exchange markets, one in Hong Kong and one in Shanghai, with different exchange rates and even different interest rates.

China's transition to a free floating exchange rate seemed to have started a few years ago. Then the stock market shocks - with related capital outflows - convinced Xi to restore controls on capital outflows.

What is the dollar today? Why has the centrality of this currency withstood the relative decline of the American empire? How long can his supremacy last? These are questions that the whole world has been asking on and off since the 1970s. Today the mechanism of the infernal trap that seems to be pushing America and China towards confrontation on many terrains raises questions about the "exorbitant privilege" of the dollar. On the fact, for example, that the United States can print at will knowing that the rest of the world "must" accept them. And then the United States itself can subject other countries – precisely by virtue of the fact that they use their dollar – to economic sanctions decided and applied unilaterally. Europe, despite being linked by friendship and alliance treaties with the United States, has repeatedly shown signs of intolerance towards the domination of the dollar (since the days of Charles De Gaulle). Let alone China, now that the climate of a new cold war is poisoning its relations with the other superpower.

To talk about the dollar, I'll try to follow the journey of one of these banknotes, some real and some virtual, given that digital means of payment are replacing them today. An American consumer enters a Walmart hypermarket in Texas and buys a radio set. Obviously it is made in China. That simple gesture is the beginning of a journey that transports dollars around the planet. In the next step, the green banknotes are transferred from the Chinese company to its central bank; the latter uses dollars to finance investments in Nigeria's natural resources. African country spends hard currency to buy rice from India. Who buys oil from Iraq. From Baghdad, a payment for weapons made in Russia starts. A Russian oligarch exports capital to Germany, from Frankfurt a German pension fund places it in London. A British company hunts for opportunities in the US market. In the end, the green banknote returns to the hands of the initial consumer: who works as a doorman in a hotel and sees it delivered (returned?) as a tip by a passing customer.

This "around the world in 80 days" à la Jules Verne, with a piece of paper instead of the intrepid traveler Phileas Fogg, is the literary device devised by the English economist Dharshini David to tell the role of money in the global economy, reveal the arcana, highlight the problems, in the book *The world in a dollar. The journey of a banknote from Texas to China, from Nigeria to Iraq to understand the global economy* (UTET, 2019). Not all transfers from one country to another involve banknotes - sometimes these are virtual dollars, transferred from a company's balance sheet to a bank and vice versa, electronic currency. Credit cards, Paypal, smartphones used as wallets, Bitcoin and Libra (Facebook's cryptocurrency), competition is becoming increasingly fierce. However, let's not underestimate paper: David recalls that «dead presidents – as the one-dollar bills with George Washington's face are called – are printed every day at the rate of 17 million, just for the one-dollar denomination; overall there are 11.7 billion greenbacks in wallets, ATMs, shop tills; and half are located outside the United States.

David is fascinated by the dollar for several reasons. "As a child, the daughter of two travellers," her parents are of Indian descent, "it struck me to see it used in every corner of the planet, from Brunei to Barbados." Then there's his passion for economics, an early university career, a job in finance in the City of London. Her academic training inspires some historical digressions, the journey of the dollar can also be done back in time: «It was not originally American, the ancestor of this word is the silver thaler used in Bohemia in the 16th century . Translated into English it becomes a dollar in Shakespeare's *Macbeth* , 1606. Dollars were used by the Spanish and Portuguese, the *conquistadors* minted them with silver from the mines of Mexico; from there to the United States, which adopted the dollar to get rid of the pound after independence, and made it the only official currency from 1792». The contemporary journey in which David guides us serves to illustrate the circularity of the world economy, the flows of liquidity and finance which are the blood system, the communicating vessels of globalisation. «The dollar» explains Davis «is not just any currency, it is also the face of American power and American interests. It has also become one of the safest ways to store valuables; it is the reserve currency of the whole world; the agent of globalization. The author recalls how many times we have heard "the decline of the dollar" prophesied, perhaps as a wish from America's rival leaders and powers.

None of these prophecies have come true so far, not even when it was China that openly supported the rise of its renminbi as an international currency. But let's be honest: who among us would like to invest their retirement money in renminbi? There is an obvious paradox, because for seventy-five years the economic, technological, political and military supremacy of the United States has undergone a constant erosion. The enormous gap that separated America from Europe or China at the end of World War II has narrowed substantially. Yet there is no currency that can compete with his. The dollar came out of anything but battered by the systemic shock of 2008. The winning therapy was printing dollars, albeit technically elaborated in a more sophisticated way with bond purchases (*quantitative easing*). By printing dollars, America has pulled itself out of the crisis and partly the others as well.

It is a story whose other side is beginning to emerge today: the risk that the party will end badly, when the liquidity machine stops. Certainly, however, we have not moved from an American monetary hegemony to a Chinese one. "The dollar is our currency but it's your problem," said John Connally, US Treasury Secretary, in 1971 when the Nixon administration decided to decouple the dollar from gold parity and plunged the world into a decade of hyperinflation. , skyrocketing rates and financial storms. It's a joke that no American executive repeats today, but one that faithfully reflects the dilemma China finds itself in. The shock therapy applied by the American central bank under the leadership of Ben Bernanke, during the Obama presidency, was decisive and worked a miraculous recovery of the global economy. In the past, attention was mainly focused on the beneficial effects for the US economy.

The economic historian Adam Tooze in the essay *Lo schianto* (Mondadori, 2018) illustrated the international dimension of that therapy. The Fed acted as the central bank of the entire world, its liquidity creation exporting credit and growth to the four corners of the planet. The Fed provided 4.5 trillion of liquidity to Europe, Asia, Latin America. Its *swap* mechanisms acted as life preservers for central banks in many emerging countries, from Brazil to Mexico, Singapore to South Korea. Ten years after the crisis, one result is that the dollar has strengthened its centrality: today it is the anchor currency for a number of countries which account for 70 per cent of world GDP, up from 60 per cent in 2008. Another finding is that much of the growth in emerging countries over the past decade has been financed by a tsunami of cheap dollar credit. The International Monetary Fund has calculated that 260 billion dollars of investments in the stock markets of emerging countries can be explained by the effects of the expansionary monetary policy practiced in Washington. His Majesty the dollar replicates the unchallenged domination that was the pound, and undermining it is not easy. Nor should we hope that this will happen until we have clear ideas on how to replace it.

These days, if one listens to the public discourse within the globalist establishment, one has an image of America as a pariah: a nation that, thanks to its president, is slipping into isolation, cutting ties with allies of all time, falling the world towards a series of catastrophes (economic, environmental), and in doing so accelerates its own decline in the first place, as well as creating serious problems for all the others. But the discourse of the globalist establishment has an internal contradiction. Capitalists vote with capital. And capital is flying to America more than ever. In just one month, June 2019, foreign investors bought US securities, stocks and bonds, for a total of 64 billion dollars. It is the highest since August 2018, it is a value that is in the very high range. It does not at all confirm the image of an isolated, struggling, declining America. On the contrary: if anything, it relaunches the theme of the American "exception", of a country that still manages to represent an oasis of stability and security in a chaotic, unpredictable world. After all, the flow of capital that floods Wall Street and Washington (the latter as the seat of the federal government which issues Treasury Bonds) is faithfully reflected in the strength of the dollar, at its all-time highs.

Various factors, some structural and others conjunctural, contribute to the irresistible attraction of the United States. Starting with the latter: the fact that in 2019 US government bonds continue to offer positive returns, albeit decreasing, while German ones are negative, plays a trivial role. Whoever puts his savings in a German Bund effectively pays the Berlin government to keep that money; whoever lends them to Uncle Sam, on the other hand, receives interest. The other economic data is the growth differential: the American economy slows down, but in 2019 it is in its tenth year of recovery and is still at a cruising speed of +2 per cent increase in GDP, while the Eurozone slips towards yet another recession. If we broaden the range of options for international investors to include Asia and emerging countries, the situation does not change much. China and Japan are the other economic giants, but both are far more vulnerable to protectionism than the United States. Exporting countries have much more to lose in the trade war.

Finally, moving on to the structural factors, still no one - certainly not China - is able to offer a capital market as liquid, as efficient, as secure as the American one. I am referring to efficiency and safety in day-to-day transactions; which does not exclude catastrophes such as that of 2008. However, the great crisis of 2008 has left us with a paradoxically strengthened role of the dollar in the world economy. China is perfectly aware that in the challenge with America it must increase its attractiveness as a financial market. He knows and tries. In September 2019, Beijing abolished all restrictions on foreign institutional investors, i.e. banks and mutual funds, hedge funds and pension funds (not to be confused with multinational industries, whose capital when they build factories are defined as "direct investments"). Previously, foreign capital was capped at $300 billion. But in reality that ceiling has never been reached, the maximum of foreign financial investments in China has reached 111 billion, just over a third of what was allowed.

There are many reasons why the world's major financial managers invest in China with caution. All are connected in some way to politics, to the nature of his authoritarian system. There is a fear of entrusting savings to a country in which the government is answerable only to itself and can tighten restrictions on capital movements at will, can manipulate the exchange rate, can intervene with dirigiste measures on stock market prices. Everything that the strength of the People's Republic has done translates into a mirror image of weakness: in the end, commandist methods allowed China to emerge unscathed from the western recession of 2008, and also allowed it to overcome the fears of the financial markets in 2015 -2016. By maintaining a less open financial system, less subject to the whims of the markets, Beijing has gained in terms of security. At the same time it confirmed all the mistrust of international investors. Added to this is the absence of a rule of law, so that in the event of disputes, a foreign investor does not know how much he will be protected: this is one of the reasons why Hong Kong has long been considered a "precious" exception for the Republic itself popular, a sort of financial free port where the criteria of Western legality apply. Finally, behind the prudence of foreign investors, there is great doubt about the opacity of Chinese finance, the amount of hidden debts, the existence of a "shadow" banking system. The Institute of International Finance has estimated that from 2005 to 2018, bank loans to Chinese companies rose from 112 to 152 percent of GDP. There is private debt that exceeds public debt, and it doesn't have the transparency we are used to in market economies.

Xi's China has so far made a choice: between the combination of freedom and instability, which is typical of American finance, and a more closed system but more controllable by the government, it has preferred the latter. The survival of the regime depends on it: if Xi leaves his citizens the total freedom to export their savings abroad, a "mistrust of money" could become the equivalent of an electoral defeat, a visible sign of loss of consensus. The closed or semi-closed model has its own internal coherence, a compelling logic. The challenge between the two parallel universes of finance, the Western and the Chinese, is another facet of the general conflict towards which we are sliding.

VIII

Hong Kong, a fragment of the West adrift

Before starting the long diplomatic negotiations for the return of the island of Hong Kong to the People's Republic, in 1982 the Chinese leader Deng Xiaoping had told the British premier Margaret Thatcher: «I could enter Hong Kong and take it by force in a single afternoon ». The Iron Lady replied, "And I couldn't stop them, but the whole world would see the true face of China." This exchange was recounted by Thatcher in her memoirs. The diplomat who headed the Chinese delegation, Lu Ping, later confirmed that dialogue and a disturbing background. In secret, Deng had ordered the People's Liberation Army to prepare plans for an invasion. The military option was seriously considered by the Beijing regime even if in parallel it was negotiating an agreed restitution of their former colony with the British. In the end, however, the same communist leader who in 1989 did not hesitate to crush the Tiananmen Square movement in blood, preferred to use kid gloves with Hong Kong.

As I write, Xi Jinping seems to have taken the same approach as Deng. Months of protests on the streets of Hong Kong, often directed against the Beijing government, have not triggered a military response. A few kilometers from Hong Kong, where the mainland and the Chinese motherland begin, Xi has sent troops and special units of riot police. However, at least until the end of September 2019, he used them sparingly, as a show of force, a threatening and dissuasive deployment, leaving it to the local police to repress the demonstrations. If a similar revolt had occurred in a city in mainland China - even worse if in Tibet or Xinjiang - there is no doubt that the response of the central authorities would have been much more rapid and violent. Why is Hong Kong still entitled to different treatment? What makes it so special? And at the same time, why has its periodic riots never infected the rest of China? Hong Kong has this ability: it surprises everyone, on a regular basis. The Chinese authorities seem taken aback every time his anger erupts. Western observers tend to overestimate its impact on the mother country. In the climate of the new cold war, the Hong Kong case is also one of the hot dossiers that spoil relations between the People's Republic and the West. We also judge Xi by how he reacts to this hotbed of instability. He judges us, observing how much we want to "interfere" in what he considers an internal matter. Finally, we are all interested (first of all Xi) in understanding whether the unrest in Hong Kong is the precursor of a wider phenomenon, or whether it is destined to remain isolated, and perhaps to fade away slowly. Until the next uprising.

I don't pretend to have certainties, but a little historical memory does. To try to shed light on the enigma of Hong Kong it is useful to remember that the former British colony is a volcano with frequent eruptions. The explosion of the square in 2019 is only the latest in a long series. My travel notebooks, the notes I kept from my reportages, year after year give me back a "historical series". It is in this chain of events that the genesis, the antecedents, the keys to interpreting the enigma can be found. Rereading my notes from many years ago gives the impression of *déjà vu* , as if the eruptions were spectacular, but always the same. In reality, observing the final conformation of the volcano, one realizes that there has been a progressive slip. The 2019 crisis resembles those that preceded it, yes. But Hong Kong is different. Its weight, its contractual strength, are no longer the same.

August 7, 2006.

Three years ago, on 1 July 2003, five hundred thousand people (almost a tenth of the entire population) took to the streets to demand real political reform. Beijing reacted with distrust and demonization. Hu Jintao declared that "anti-patriotic, anti-Chinese forces, maneuvered from abroad, were at work in Hong Kong to make the island a subversive base against the whole nation". The regime was afraid that an "orange revolution" like the ones that were shaking Ukraine and Georgia could start from Hong Kong. In 2005, the governor - who is officially called "chief executive", like the managing director of a company - Tung Chee Hwa was forced to resign and was replaced by the 62-year-old Catholic Donald Tsang Yam-kuen, trained in the British civil service, equally obedient to Beijing but more skilled in dialogue with the population.

When I return, in the summer of 2006, we are once again in an emergency: the probation of Hong Kong, the only city without censorship in authoritarian

China, risks having its days numbered. The pro-Chinese administration passed a law granting unprecedented powers to local police to spy on its citizens, including opposition politicians and journalists. Everyone can be put under surveillance with the use of electronic means such as bugging homes or email monitoring. This way Hong Kong can become a little more like Beijing and Shanghai.

The law may be the prelude to an authoritarian turnaround in the rich island city, a financial center of international importance, which until 1997 had been a British colony. In the nine years after the handover of Hong Kong to China, the Beijing government has tolerated that the city remained very different from the rest of the country: the press has not yet been subjected to a gag, the right to demonstrate and disagree is guaranteed. So far the Chinese regime has kept the commitments contained in the bilateral agreements signed by Thatcher and the communist leader Deng Xiaoping when they decided on the transfer of sovereignty. Respect for Hong Kong's diversity has always been seen as a test of the trustworthiness of popular China, especially since the island city is the largest Asian stock exchange after Tokyo, is a global banking center and is home to a large community of western businessmen. Hong Kong's freedoms are the legacy of the rule of law left by the British, but they have a limit that can prove fatal: the lack of self-government. The Chinese Communists are not wrong when they denounce the hypocrisy of the British: as long as Hong Kong was a colony, it never had the democracy that existed in London. Britain became "passionate" about the political rights of local citizens only at the time of their transfer to Chinese sovereignty. The administrative authority of the island after 1997 answers to a local Parliament that only half is elected by the citizens; the other half are appointed by socioeconomic and professional corporations, which effectively serve as a transmission belt for Beijing's influence.

The consequences of limited sovereignty are measured in this summer of 2006. The legislative assembly has approved a potentially liberticidal law. The legislation makes espionage of citizens and any form of electronic surveillance by the police constitutional. It was the epilogue of a frantic parliamentary battle, unprecedented in the history of Hong Kong: 57 and a half hours of session with a tenacious obstructionism of the democratic opposition, which presented two hundred amendments. Governor Donald Tsang tried to reassure his fellow citizens by declaring that "the new system of rules is as good as those in force in the most democratic jurisdictions in the world". Police chief Lee Siu-kwong called the reform "an important law for maintaining order and security." However, it is not clear that order and security are in danger in Hong Kong. The city does not have high crime rates. Notable criminal activities are linked to the Triads, which are known to collude with pieces of the Chinese nomenklatura in the neighboring Guangdong region.

This is not the threat that Beijing cares about. The communist regime is annoyed by the fact that demonstrations for democracy are held regularly in Hong Kong, or in honor of the students massacred in Tiananmen Square in 1989. Furthermore, the free Hong Kong press has become the preferred medium for those Chinese who want to disseminate news prohibited in their country. In Guangdong, whenever there are workers' strikes or peasant protests, activists call Hong Kong reporters. And since Hong Kong has been an integral part of the People's Republic, Chinese tourism on the island has grown exponentially. If Beijing does not normalize Hong Kong, could the anomalous city one day "infect" the rest of the country? In addition to the many citizens eager to maintain their freedom, there is still a fabric of civil servants trained under British administration in Hong Kong who resist Chinese normalization. But networks of policemen and spies from Beijing have been operating in secret on the island for some time, and their activity has become increasingly intense in recent years. The Chinese government nervously followed the massive demonstrations of 2003, when a large part of the city took to the streets to demand "true" elections, i.e. the right to vote to elect all deputies. It is a democratic tear that Beijing has always postponed, to maintain control over the island and not create dangerous precedents for the rest of the country.

March 25, 2007.

When CNN programs in China experience blackouts, something interesting is happening. For the past few days, the American network's news has had sudden gaps - artfully caused by the technology of Beijing's censors - every time they cover the Hong Kong elections. Today, in fact, for the first time in history, the former British island votes according to "almost" democratic rules to elect its governor.

In reality, the result is obvious. Beijing's favorite man, outgoing governor Donald Tsang, has victory in his pocket. According to Hong Kong's complicated political system, it is not the 7 million resident citizens who can choose the governor. This power is in the hands of 800 "big voters", who in theory should represent the citizenry, in fact they are chosen above all in the financial, industrial and commercial circles with ties to China. The small parliament of big voters is therefore heavily influenced by the Beijing government.

However, even with these limitations, Hong Kong's desire for democracy is felt at every level. For the first time, today's poll is a real ballot: as many as 132 of the 800 electors have designated Tsang's rival, the Democratic lawyer Alan Leong, in advance, who can therefore challenge the outgoing governor in a duel. Another novelty is just as significant. Tsang himself tried to answer the demand for participation that comes from below (in all polls it emerges that 60 percent of the population wants a complete democracy). In a recent interview with the foreign press he promised that within five years he will propose political reforms to satisfy the thirst for representation. It is not clear how he will be able to do this without displeasing his contacts in Beijing. Tsang showed courage when he noted that people in neighboring Guangdong look up to the privileged rights of the former British colony. He also said that when Hong Kong TVs - free from any censorship - went to interview the people of Guangdong, they were often asked: "Why can't we Chinese choose our governors like you do?". Tsang's press conference was also conveniently blacked out by the TV networks of the People's Republic.

Hong Kong's political system is a strange hybrid, the fruit of many compromises. When the island was administered by the United Kingdom, the local governor was appointed from London and there was no representative democracy. However, there was a rule of law, an independent judiciary, freedom of the press. Hong Kong continues to have an autonomous law and court system (legal certainty is important, among other things, for its credibility as an international financial centre). Tsang in 1989 could afford to sharply criticize the crackdown in Tiananmen Square. In Hong Kong, Cardinal Joseph Zen Ze-kiun, the Catholic prelate who fights for human rights and freedom of religion in China, enjoys maximum freedom of speech. Furthermore, the population of Hong Kong, while they would like a representative democracy without the current limits and conditions, seem to appreciate the material benefits offered by the Beijing government. Thanks to the boom in Chinese tourism that flows to the island to shop, thanks to the development of business with the motherland and with the numerous Chinese multinationals that are listed on the local stock exchange, Hong Kong's economy is bursting with health.

There is a collateral cost of this prosperity, which the people of Hong Kong bear less and less: appalling environmental degradation. At the last Hong Kong marathon, hundreds of runners were hospitalized due to illness due to toxic dust in the air. Many Western cruise ships stopping in the port cancel a visit to the Peak – the top of the mountain which is a traditional tourist attraction – because the view from above over Hong Kong Bay is hidden by a thick blanket of smog. Some Western multinationals have had to offer their expatriate managers in Hong Kong special health allowances for the risks of respiratory diseases. Tsang, defying once again the wrath of Beijing, accuses the factories of nearby Guangdong, and above all the Chinese coal-fired power plants, for the dramatic environmental deterioration of the island. However, his democratic rival Leong has thrown an inconvenient truth in his face: many factories in Guangdong that today spew their carbon emissions into the Hong Kong sky (or their toxic sewage into the waters of the Pearl River Delta) are owned by tycoons from the island, who got rich by relocating to the nearby People's Republic where wages are much lower and worker protection non-existent.

May 1, 2007 in the «sister» island, Macao.

China's May Day, China's most important national holiday, was marred by a flare of social unrest where no one expected it: in Macao, the former Portuguese colony that is Asia's gambling Mecca. Flooded by money from the casino industry, the island enjoys an autonomous status like Hong Kong, and in recent years has been talked about for only two reasons: the business boom and suspicions of money laundering. Suddenly the other side of the economic miracle was discovered: growing unemployment, fueled by the influx of underpaid Chinese labour, and the corruption of the local administration controlled by Beijing.

Discontent exploded on Labor Day. While the rest of China was on vacation for a week (150 million travelers on the most popular "bridge" of the year), in Macao the police fired on the crowd and narrowly missed tragedy. It all started when a demonstration of ten thousand people approached the home of chief executive Ho Hau-wah, who governs Macao under the watchful eye of the Chinese regime. The march, made up largely of unemployed workers and bricklayers, was met by a massive deployment of riot police. Shots were fired from the special police squads. The shots unleashed exasperation in the procession, for five hours the city remained in a state of siege, devastated by violent clashes. After countless chases and beatings, tear gas and rubber bullets, the police finally managed to regain control. The official toll is only ten arrests and twenty-one injured among the policemen, but many demonstrators were saved by avoiding hospitals, to prevent their arrest. Among the banners that appeared at the head of the demonstration, and which the police immediately destroyed, one read "Communist party, give us back justice". At the end of the day of clashes, the police chief denounced "a real riot", the local government condemned "the criminal incidents".

This bloody May Day has revealed the social rift that is widening in the heart of an apparently prosperous city. Since Macao became part of China again (in 1999, two years after Hong Kong), the former Portuguese colony has not stood out for its political sensitivity. Unlike Hong Kong, the sister island seemed content with economic benefits. The People's Republic, in fact, has encouraged the boom of the casino industry, to control its dividends. Gambling is very popular among the Chinese, but it remains prohibited in their country, which has led to a proliferation of border casinos in all neighboring countries, from Vietnam to North Korea. To avoid the outflow of capital, Beijing has given carte blanche to the Macao authorities on the gaming business, and in a few years the island has multiplied its casinos to the point of stealing the world record from Las Vegas. Leading this expansion is the Sands Casino group, repeatedly accused of corruption and collusion with the local government.

Macau's banking system is also a gray area where anything is possible. Last year a local bank was identified as the main tool for the money laundering by Kim Jong-il, the North Korean dictator. Beijing turns a blind eye, thus reinforcing the suspicion that the regime is in favor of an "offshore square" of this nature. But the gambling-driven economic boom does not benefit the islanders equally. While Macao's GDP has increased by 60 per cent in the last three years, ie at twice the rate of Chinese growth, inflation is galloping and unemployment is rising.

Adding to the discontent is the casino's recruitment policy. In just a few months, the Sands group alone imported 70,000 employees from mainland China to take advantage of cheaper labour. Competition from the Chinese depresses local wages. Macao society appears as a faithful mirror of its new urban physiognomy. The city, in fact, is more and more clearly divided. On one side, the districts of ultra-modern and vulgar skyscrapers that house luxury hotels and gambling halls. On the other, the old Portuguese city, sleepy and depressed, with its beautiful Baroque monuments that decompose in the sun, abandoned like the ruins of a past that does not interest the new masters.

June 26, 2007.

I return to Hong Kong on the tenth anniversary of the transition from Great Britain to China. Balance moment. This decade has not been easy for Her Majesty's former colony.

The chronicle of this period is a series of mishaps, shocks and fears. A few hours have passed since that July 1, 1997, the Royal Yacht *Britannia* has just set sail from the port with Prince Charles of England and the last governor Chris Patten on board, when dramatic turbulence is looming on the horizon. The day after the handover, Hong Kong bankers learn that Thailand, bleeding from capital flight, devalues the baht, its national currency. It is the initial detonator of the great Asian crisis. One after another in the autumn of 1997 the "dragons" are hit by the waves of international speculation. Indonesia and Malaysia have to capitulate in turn, the domino effect knocks down the currencies of the area like many skittles. Hong Kong's central bank defends itself with the strength of desperation, raising interest rates up to 18.5 percent in order to keep the local dollar pegged to the American one. It fails to prevent a 60 percent fall in the stock market, the collapse of the real estate market (half of the value of homes pulverized in a few months), tripled unemployment, a deflation that will last three years. Warning sign: the only anchor of stability amidst the panic in Southeast Asia is Beijing, which resisted devaluation in 1997 and prevented the crisis from spreading further.

Three years later, the Hong Kong Stock Exchange has almost recovered from its slump when the New Economy "bubble" on Wall Street bursts, dragging Asian telecom and overvalued dot-com stocks with it. Then it was the turn of 11 September 2001, with the long paralysis of air transport particularly harmful for Hong Kong, a tourist city and airport "hub" in the Far East. Finally, the Sars epidemic in 2003, a poisoned gift from the People's Republic given that the incubation took place in Guangdong and was hidden by the silence of the local health authorities. Once again, the blow is harder for Hong Kong: the island thrives on commerce and congresses, its intercontinental airport is deserted for months, the hotels have 90 percent of the rooms empty, the shopping malls are abandoned by international customers .

It is at that point that the Chinese regime realizes it needs to launch a lifeline. Unexpected aid arrives from Beijing: the government liberalizes tourism from the motherland, offers generous relief for bilateral trade. As soon as the terror of SARS passed, the turnout of the nouveau riche Chinese exploded. Hong Kong is invaded from all sides: the middle-upper class of Beijing and Shanghai come for weekend shopping, the wealthiest also invest in the real estate market; Westerners bet on the island's stock exchange hoping to reap the fruits of the impetuous rise of the new capitalist China there.

In 2005, the financial center of Hong Kong surpassed both New York and London for the value of placements of new listed companies. In 2006, it was here that the largest placement in world history up to that point was made, the listing of the Industrial and Commercial Bank of China for $22 billion. Lee Shau Kee, one of the richest capitalists on the island, expresses the mercantile and materialistic soul of Hong Kong when he says: «I've never been passionate about politics. I'm only interested in the economy. I look at the balance sheet of these ten years under the Chinese government, and I say that we can be satisfied. We don't need protests. We live in a harmonious society, as President Hu Jintao says." The democratic movement defends freedom tooth and nail, every June 4th it commemorates the dead in Tiananmen Square, and continues to call for real elections. By order of Beijing, Tsang stalls and postpones any reform to a very distant horizon. Political science professor Willy Wo-Lap Lam says: «In cinema and pop-music, we in Hong Kong have made inroads into the mass culture of China. But as far as tainting our liberal values into the reform debate in Beijing, the relationship between Hong Kong and the motherland is one of David versus Goliath. A Chinese-sized Goliath."

October 5, 2007.

The green and tranquil oasis of Victoria Park is a good place to see what makes Hong Kong a Chinese city different from the rest of China. Around this park that could be in central London, everywhere you look you see indelible imprints of the British style inherited from the colonial period. Double-decker buses. Bankers' clubs with mahogany-walled smoking rooms and bay windows. The cosmopolitan elegance of ladies in tea rooms. The refined design of the skyscrapers designed by Sir Norman Foster and Ieoh Ming Pei. Above all, there is the culture of freedom and human rights, which attracts thousands of demonstrators to Victoria Park every year to protest on the anniversary of the Tiananmen Square massacre.

But here near the park, in the palaces of power, Governor Tsang has another vision. For him, the winning metropolis of the 21st century is like a multinational competing on the global market, a *brand* to be imposed to attract capital, human talent, ideas and innovations. Therefore the island of Hong Kong with its 7 million inhabitants is close to him. Tsang has decided to launch a takeover bid on another gigantic metropolis, its twin city on the mainland: Shenzhen, 10 million inhabitants, the beating heart of Chinese industrial power. The marriage proposal is now official. The project is to build a megalopolis bigger than New York, London, Tokyo. The symbol of the merger has just been inaugurated, it's called the Hong Kong - Shenzhen Western Corridor, an immense highway bridge that quadruples the road traffic flow between the two cities. The high-speed train and ultra-fast metro between the two international airports will soon follow. «It will be a tool at the service of

Chinese power in the world» proclaims the official project of the experts of the Bauhinia Foundation, a think tank at the service of the municipality of Hong Kong. "I've been admiring Hong Kong for years and trying to learn from her," her boyfriend replied enthusiastically: Xu Zongheng, the mayor of Shenzhen.

It is difficult to imagine two more different betrothed. On the one hand there is Hong Kong, the aristocrat with snobbish exoticism, the financial city of Asia, the bridge between East and West. On the other is Shenzhen, which thirty years ago was still a fishing village, invisible on maps. Shenzhen is an invention of Deng, Mao's *de facto* successor who renounced Maoism. At the end of the 1970s, old Deng launched the experiment of «special economic zones», free ports where private initiative was encouraged, liberalization eliminated the bonds and snares of communist dirigisme, Western investments were welcome. Today Shenzhen is the "boomtown" par excellence, a 1930s Chicago projected into the global economy, a monstrous agglomeration of skyscrapers and factories, where worker exploitation in concentration camps coexists side by side with high technology poles and scientific research that they make a Chinese Silicon Valley.

The idea of launching this urban takeover bid was born in Hong Kong because it is the richest: over 30,000 US dollars in annual per capita income, a standard of living three times higher than its neighbour. But economic growth in Hong Kong is 6 percent annually, in Shenzhen 15 percent. Hong Kong has an aging skilled workforce, Shenzhen offers a "reserve army" with Chinese wages, a population that dreams of the quality of education and social services of the former British colony. Hong Kong can only develop in height, surrounded by the sea and limited by mountains, Shenzhen has a land area twice as large. It is the ideal union between two complementary forces. «Together» predicts Tsang «we will have 3200 square kilometers of territory, soon we will reach twenty million inhabitants, more than the greater New York (Manhattan, Brooklyn, Bronx, Newark).» With two of the largest naval ports in the world and the busiest intercontinental airport in all of Asia. It is, in a sense, as one might imagine a marriage of Los Angeles and Mexico City: cinematic glamor and workforce, high finance and mass demographic. In the ranking of gross domestic product, the new megalopolis Hong Kong - Shenzhen will have overtaken London and Paris by 2020. Eight months of study, extensive consultations between the entrepreneurs of the two cities, a task force of 300 municipal officials were enough, and the project was launched.

Like any marriage, this too must be able to bring together different characters. The unknowns are many. The autonomy regime has allowed Hong Kong to "select" to a certain extent what it wants to take from the People's Republic and what it prefers to keep at a distance. There is still a customs post between the island and the mainland. Citizens of the People's Republic cannot automatically obtain residence and work permits in the former British colony. The currency is different and pegged to the US dollar. The unions of the island fear the invasion of a docile and underpaid workforce, a "social dumping". Faithful to its image of the "new Chicago", Shenzhen with the boom in wealth has bred a powerful crime: kidnappings for the purpose of extortion. The Hong Kong Democratic Foundation has defined the ideal conditions for the union: "It's a very good idea as long as it creates a Greater Hong Kong, not a Greater Shenzhen. The integration must extend the rule of law, the culture of civil responsibility, the reduction of corruption and crime to Shenzhen". It is a generous and utopian proclamation, which ignores the relationship of forces: behind Shenzhen there is the People's Republic with its one billion four hundred million inhabitants, an authoritarian regime, the largest army on the planet, a formidable censorship apparatus. For now, the local government of Hong Kong puts the political problem in brackets. It hides behind the ambiguous slogan "one country, two systems", the same one that has guaranteed the fragile diversity of the island in these ten years.

Meanwhile, the preparations for the wedding proceed at a rapid pace: the hyper-fast connection by rail, the interconnection between the airports. A visa-free entry lane for two million Shenzhen citizens will soon be tested. Behind Shenzhen is then Guangzhou (formerly Canton), another metropolis with over ten million inhabitants. The high-speed rail will reduce the commute time to Guangzhou from the current three hours to just 45 minutes. Hong Kong capitalists are already traveling the world "selling" their city as the management center of all of Guangdong, as the thinking brain of a region which is the factory of the planet. They are in a hurry to celebrate the wedding, because this idea already has followers and important rivals. Hong Kong's eternal competitor, Shanghai, extends its tentacles towards Nanjing and Hangzhou: together the three cities reach 30 million inhabitants. Further north, Beijing strengthens ties with its landlocked Tianjing: their integration creates a shock mass of 25 million inhabitants. In the rest of the world, these figures give shivers, evoke nightmares of congestion, social ungovernability, environmental collapse. Even in China there is no lack of voices of alarm. But the leaders feel the irresistible charm of gigantism, they remain convinced that size is power.

I reread my description of that supercity project twelve years later. History has taken a very different path. The megacities of Guangdong today no longer have any inferiority complex towards Hong Kong. On the contrary. It is the former British island that has experienced the greatest difficulties, a decline that has made it weaker. Guangzhou and Shenzhen in 2019 look down on it. Hong Kong has not changed much in these twelve years, in the sense that the level of freedom and legal certainty remain much higher than in the Chinese motherland. It remains an important financial center and this justifies Xi's prudence, who is hesitant to break the precious toy. But the rest of the world has changed: the strength of China and its self-awareness under Xi, the attitude of America and the West.

Among the many protests that have shaken Hong Kong in recent years - in 2003, in 2012, in 2014 - the one that exploded in 2019 is the most massive and prolonged. Initially one million citizens took to the streets: one for every seven residents of the island. Then popular participation decreased. Radical, violent elements have taken over, somewhat similar to our "black blocks". The processions have become smaller, mainly by young people. It could be one of the most desperate protests. In the sense that in Beijing there is a regime more determined than ever to tame it. While the attitude of the West is even more ambiguous than in the past. With the typical reflection of authoritarian regimes, and a script tested since the days of the "Orange Revolutions", the American conspiracy is also a convenient theory to explain the Hong Kong protest. Beijing's government media allude to Washington's hand behind the mass mobilization. On the contrary, what is happening in Hong Kong arouses increasingly feeble protests in the West.

Since Xi Jinping has been in charge of Beijing, raids by Chinese police against Hong Kong dissidents have become more frequent. Some were literally kidnapped, disappeared for a long time, only to reappear in the hands of the Chinese authorities and perhaps make Stalinist-style "self-denunciations". The initial spark of the 2019 uprising was a reform of the extradition law (later withdrawn) which would have made the task even easier for the Chinese police: they would no longer need to organize kidnappings, the Hong Kong authorities would have hand over the dissidents to her. The street protests have won. At least on this one. At least for now.

The Cassandras who feared the end of the Hong Kong anomaly were proven wrong until September 2019. But for how long? Those in the West who deluded themselves about a democratic contagion from the island to the continent were wrong, as were those in Beijing who feared it. One fact is significant. As I visited China again in the summer of 2019, information about the Hong Kong protests was tightly controlled by government censorship. The citizens of Beijing and Shanghai were kept in the dark for the first few months. Then the Chinese government began to spread images of violent clashes: alternating between condemnations of young thugs in action and denunciations of an American conspiracy that allegedly incited them. But this state information does not have a monopoly on news in Guangdong's two neighboring megacities. Shenzhen and Guangzhou are so close to the border that everyone receives free-to-air Hong Kong TV programs. Yet there have been no transfers of protests on that side of the border, nor signs of solidarity or sympathy. Zero contagion; just like in the previous installments. The impression is that for many Guangdong residents, Hong Kong protesters are spoiled, selfish and unpatriotic kids.

Another interesting and new data is the socio-economic dimension of the protest. Even as China grew richer and richer, the plight of Hong Kong's younger generation worsened. On the one hand, they suffer from downward wage competition from their peers who come from the Chinese motherland. On the other hand, the cost of living in Hong Kong, linked to building income, has gone crazy. The real estate speculation tycoons – the ones the Xi regime can rely on – have stripped the city. For young people, if they are not scions of capitalist dynasties, the future is gray. From this point of view, the 2019 protest does not oppose Hong Kong to the People's Republic, but reveals an internal rift between two Hong Kongs. This could encourage Xi Jinping to adopt a wait-and-see tactic, betting on the victory of the very rich against the impoverished youth of their dreams.

The only comforting lesson from the Hong Kong affair is this: we have the confirmation that there is no cultural, let alone "genetic" incompatibility between the Chinese and liberal democracy. This, moreover, has been demonstrated for many years by the democratic experience of Taiwan, whose citizens observe the events in Hong Kong with particular attention and apprehension. If Xi does not respect Hong Kong's autonomy, it is not credible that he would preserve democratic freedoms in the event of Taiwan's reunification with the motherland.

However, the younger generations of Hong Kong have something that distinguishes them from the Taiwanese. In addition to the attachment to political freedoms, they have developed a "hybrid" identity, full of contaminations between East and West. They feel Chinese but are also proud of an ideal heritage inherited from Great Britain, and have grown up in close connection with American culture. This was their strength in the past. Today, in the climate of the new cold war, it is not certain that there will remain as much space for these "ambiguous" identities.

Conclusion

If you know the enemy and know yourself, your victory is sure. If you know yourself but not your enemy, your odds of winning and losing are equal. If you don't know the enemy and you don't know yourself, you will succumb in every battle.

SUN TZU, *The Art of War*, 6th century BC

A section of our ruling classes has stuck to an antiquated idea of China as an emerging power whose commercial penetration is based on low labor costs. Too ignorant or provincial, many Western elites have underestimated one of the most far-reaching events in the history of our time: the last ten years of the frantic rush towards modernization, in which China has transformed itself into a very different "thing", until overtaking the United States in some advanced technologies. Meanwhile, Europe - out of opportunism, and the weaknesses of its capitalism - has begun to sell itself by auction to Chinese finance. But always with vague ideas about the nature of capitalism that came from the East. As for Chinese penetration in Africa and Latin America, it is the subject of superficial curiosity, clichés, clichés, generic hostility. New colonialism, looting of resources: labels that say everything and nothing, avoid the trouble of investigating. Even less was the intention to delve into the meaning of Xi Jinping's institutional coup, which overturned the Constitution of the People's Republic to appoint himself emperor for life.

Wars can break out by mistake, by misunderstanding, by miscalculation of the opponent's motivations and reactions. Perhaps the most tragic case was the First World War. Australian historian Christopher Clark coined the image of 'sleepwalking' leaders who walked into conflict without really being aware of it. The early stages of the US-China trade war – albeit less serious and bloodless – have already seen many mistakes in deciphering the adversary. From one side to the other. The Western press has especially raged on Trump's mistakes, it has followed with the usual conformism to the single neoliberal thought, which condemns all forms of protectionism. There was no shortage of errors of judgment on the part of the Chinese leadership. Sometimes disconcerting.

After all, we admire the professional caliber and technocratic depth of that leadership. Furthermore, those who govern in Beijing have two enormous advantages over us: first, they don't have to chase after electoral consensus within a few years, so they can draw up long-term plans; second, it has an enormous mass of information about our rulers, who are "open books" compared to them. Still, Xi had convinced himself that Hillary Clinton would be a far worse president for Chinese interests; he did not take seriously the protectionist proclamations of America First that Trump shouted at the top of his lungs in all the rallies. Xi has repeatedly overestimated his ability to bring the US economy to its knees. He bet on Trump's weakness, without understanding that even in the event of impeachment or electoral defeat, other Republicans or Democrats who are not at all pro-Chinese will replace him.

Of course, it is easy for China's leaders to exploit the vulnerabilities of liberal democracies: Looking at the US election cycle, Xi has focused his tariffs against sectors such as Midwestern agricultural commodities, so as to maximize the damage to a Trump electoral constituency such as *the farmers* . These are easy games for an authoritarian regime, against which a democracy cannot reciprocate: Xi does not need the votes of his citizens to be re-elected. However, with all the cognitive means at his disposal, from reading our free press to Beijing's spy network, he has not been able to decipher the root causes of Western populism, he has not seen the link between globalization and the social unease that leads to nationalism . For a Chinese leader who has sent his daughter to study at Harvard, that's not an exciting balance sheet. Deciphering Trump isn't easy, of course, especially as he prides himself on his unpredictability as a negotiating tactic. But Beijing's countless miscalculations cast a shadow on the efficiency of that regime. Or do they mean that we are missing something about the internal constraints and decision-making mechanisms of the People's Republic?

In fact, it is amazing how little Westerners are curious about a key figure of our time like Xi Jinping. The figure of Vladimir Putin in comparison is much more familiar to Italians or Americans; his biographies abound. Yet Russia is an economic dwarf, it will eventually be sucked into China's orbit. Putin's foreign policy is also partly conditioned by the logic of this new cold war: having alienated Western consensus in Crimea and Ukraine, the Russian president has no alternative but to rely on Xi's economic protectorate. Sino-Russian military cooperation is getting closer, creating new threats for NATO in the future. However, Russia too is caught in the suffocating embrace of its eastern neighbour. In the Beijing-Moscow combination, the balance of forces is reversed compared to the 1950s when they were the two capitals of communism. Today China is the master, even with its investments in the Russian energy sector. In short, it is clear who is number one and who is number two. Despite this, information on Putin's plots abounds even on our television talk shows; while its stronger partner remains a mysterious object.

The first thing we have to study about Xi is his life. At least in part he told it, with an interesting wealth of detail. Joe Biden, when he was vice president with Barack Obama in the White House, met Xi Jinping in 2011 during a trip to Beijing and Chengdu. At that time Xi was already the leader *in pectore* , his rise to power would have taken place in the following year but it was already announced. In official meetings with the American delegation, Xi was generous with details about his personal history, which is quite rare among Chinese leaders who have reached that hierarchical level. Biden and his companions recall how long Xi had taken in telling his father's story.

Xi Jinping belongs to that category that the Chinese call "little princes": he is the son of a senior leader of the communist nomenklatura, he is the exponent of a "hereditary" ruling class. Sons of art, to use a positive expression. Recommended, privileged, living proof of a nepotism that undermines the meritocratic image of the regime. As a child, Xi attended one of the elite schools reserved for the children of high communist dignitaries. When he went to visit his father, he entered the Zhongnanhai precinct, the inaccessible residence of the big bosses and party headquarters. Xi exhibits his hereditary lineage to turn it into a positive fact. For him it constitutes a sort of direct line that connects him to the epic story of the founding fathers, Mao's companions in revolutionary battles. In perfect coherence with the many references to the Celestial Empire, a "dynastic" legitimacy emerges. But what strikes us Westerners the most is perhaps another aspect. Xi's father was also a victim of the worst excesses of Maoism, he was persecuted, and his son also suffered from it. That those vicissitudes have strengthened the current president's attachment to the role of the Communist Party says a lot about his personality.

One of the few authoritative biographies of Xi Jinping is the work of an Australian colleague: Richard McGregor, correspondent of the Financial Times in Beijing and Shanghai from 2000 to 2009, now a researcher at a Sydney think tank, the Lowy Institute. Central to this book (*Xi Jinping: The Backlash* , Penguin Books Australia, 2019) is the figure of the father, Xi Zhongxun, a revolutionary militant who was among Mao's loyalists at the time of the partisan war and then at the founding of the People's Republic in 1949. Vice premier at the end of the 1950s, Xi father fell into disgrace during the ferocious Maoist purges of 1962. Then came the Cultural Revolution, another period of excesses instigated by Mao. Father Xi was humiliated by the Red Guards and ended up in prison. The parent's fall into disgrace had repercussions on his son, who was also persecuted, then exiled to the countryside at the age of 17 like many young people of his generation, forced to learn the work of the fields. Xi Jinping was forced, as was the custom in the cruel rites of that time, to pronounce a public condemnation of his father. Xi Zhongxun, according to McGregor's biography, was rehabilitated only after Mao's death. He was a moderate, like Zhou Enlai and Deng Xiaoping, two other trusted collaborators of Mao who fell into disgrace and were persecuted at various times in their lives.

From those tragic stories Xi Jinping has not drawn the slightest critical detachment towards the history of Maoism. On the contrary, if he told this familiar story at length to the American visitor Biden, it is because he considers himself tempered by life's hardships, but by no means disillusioned. His respect and admiration for Mao remain intact. Xi, in this sense, is a true communist. I know this definition may sound strange, applied to the leader of a capitalist superpower, a China teeming with billionaires and multimillionaires, and where social inequalities between rich and poor reach American levels. Xi is not an egalitarian communist, for sure; nor does his communism provide for "power to the people." But he is an authentic communist in his attachment to the primacy of the party, in the identification between party and state, in the belief that only the party is the interpreter of the true national interest. In the economic field, even without feeling absurd nostalgia for the misery imposed by Mao's choices, the current president is wary of liberal reformers and defends the role of state companies. He recently strengthened the role of Communist Party committees within private enterprises. His Australian biographer argues that not only have we Westerners misunderstood Xi, but some of his party comrades have also misunderstood him, who did not understand to what extent he was an old communist – authoritarian, centralizing, ruthless with internal enemies – when they supported his rise to the top. The "social credit" system with which it assigns scores to citizens (and can sanction them with the loss of bank credit and even deny them access to air transport) has clear Maoist ancestry.

Xi is one of the Chinese leaders who have carefully studied the story of Mikhail Gorbachev and the dissolution of the Soviet Union that followed his reforms. The introduction of partial transparency and some changes in a (cautiously) democratic sense were Gorbachev's fatal mistakes that Xi does not forgive him. At the same time, in his rise to power Xi has seen signs of political and moral decay in the Chinese Communist Party and in the power apparatuses (army, police, secret services, state companies). He decided that it was necessary to react with the utmost hardness and determination: both to reclaim the nomenklatura and to strengthen its command.

A key step in Xi's rise to power is the ignominious overthrow of his rival Bo Xilai in 2012. He was one of the party's top leaders, entrusted with the government of the world's largest megacity, that gigantic industrial conurbation of Chongqing exceeded 30 million inhabitants. Bo Xilai at the height of his power was considered an aspirant to the highest office: party secretary and president of the Republic. He had organized a sort of electoral campaign, he had promoted his notoriety with an almost Western style of communication: an investment in his own image, completely unusual in a political system where it is not the citizens but the party leaders themselves who decide the appointments.

Arrested and tried in 2012, Bo Xilai was exposed to public contempt. The accusations against him received exceptional publicity, also anomalous with respect to the tradition of washing dirty clothes in the family. In the remote past, at the end of Maoism, there had been highly visible political trials: the most famous was the trial against the conspiracy of the Gang of Four, a powerful clan to which Mao's widow belonged. But in post-Maoist China, marked by collegiate leadership and the rejection of the "cult of personality," the party tended to discipline its black sheep discreetly, sheltered from popular curiosity. For Bo Xilai, however, the fall from grace was accompanied by a national and international publicity campaign about his misdeeds.

According to the accusations that the same government leveled at him after having dismissed and indicted him, Bo was a sort of "warlord", he used the local police as his private militia, to terrorize his political opponents, blackmail and plunder entrepreneurs. Added to this was the 19th-century *noir saga* of the tiger wife, Gu Kailai. Accused of having had her English lover (who had been an accomplice in crimes and thefts) poisoned with cyanide by a servant, she was sentenced to death. The sentence was later commuted, today the husband and wife are serving life sentences. In that 2012 America was fascinated by the Chinese "thriller" which suddenly exposed the secrets of an impenetrable regime, the vices of the communist oligarchy, together with an exotic plot of forbidden love, unbridled luxury, murders. And espionage?

A tail of the scandal lapped the reputation of the most prestigious American university, Harvard. It is in this university of excellence, in the most exclusive of its faculties – the John F. Kennedy School of Government where management theories are applied to governance and public administration – that the son of the deposed communist hierarch studied. Twenty-four years old at the time, Bo Guagua ended up in all the American newspapers and magazines, photographed in night parties, or at the table of luxurious restaurants, embraced by attractive blondes. The Beijing press seized on his nocturnal deeds - "he urinated on a university fence, in a drunken state" - and on his Facebook page, as an example of a decadent lifestyle. The father tried to defend himself: "It's not true that my son drives a Ferrari, and as for the Harvard tuition I don't pay for it, he deserved a scholarship". The annual cost of attending the School of Government is $90,000, a bit too much for the official salary of even a high-ranking Communist official. On the scholarship, Harvard's academic authorities fell into an embarrassed silence. Respect for privacy... They added that in providing grants to students, the superfaculty adopts a "holistic" approach that takes into account not only academic talent but also "leadership potential". Elsewhere this "holistic" approach would be called opportunism or servility towards the scions of foreign VIPs who bring high-ranking networks of relationships as a dowry. As for the Ferrari: to be precise, Bo Guagua drove it in Beijing the evening he went to pick up the daughter of the American ambassador for a gallant appointment. At Harvard, his classmates say, he could be seen behind the wheel of a Porsche. At Harvard itself in those years there were other Chinese "princelings". The most prominent was Xi Mingze, the daughter of Xi Jinping. The girl was more cautious: she almost always used a false name, and never had a Facebook page.

Harvard was only part of the "American connection" in the most serious Chinese scandal in many decades. The spectacular fall of the powerful Bo Xilai involved the Obama administration in an accident. On 6 February 2012, the US consulate in Chengdu, in the province of Sichuan, welcomed a very particular "political refugee". To seek asylum from American diplomats was Wang Lijun, deputy mayor of the megalopolis of Chongqing and former right-hand man of Bo Xilai. Wang was the real police chief of Chongqing, the man who for years indulged Bo in his ferocious methods for his rise to power and wealth. But what happened "inside" the US consulate in Chengdu is a disconcerting event, perhaps unrepeatable today, seven years later and in the climate of a new cold war. The consulate immediately alerted the US embassy in Beijing; from there the story was reported to the White House. And the refugee instead of enjoying protection was handed over to the police of his country. That February 6 in which the superpoliceman Wang went to surrender himself to American diplomats was only a week away from the state visit of the future Chinese number one in Washington, Xi Jinping. The US right insinuated that Obama had "sold out" a high-ranking defector of strategic interest to the Americans, in order not to jeopardize the summit.

We may never know how well-founded the accusations against Bo were, or if instead his criminal parable was in part scripted by the future leader who wanted to clear the field of a rival. (If one day China adopted the rules of transparency of many Western democracies, it would open its state archives within a certain deadline: but the wait could be long.) Of course, the simple fact that for many Chinese the revelations on Bo were found to be likely says a lot about the level of corruption that had been reached.

In Xi Jinping's history that seems to be a turning point. On the one hand, Bo's fall paves the way for him to absolute power and sends a tremendous signal to his internal rivals. On the other hand, Xi seems to be convinced that the metastasis of corruption is at a critical level, that the future of the party is in danger, that extreme remedies must be adopted. The two-year period 2011-2012 is also crucial because it is the apogee of the Arab Spring and in Russia there are protests against electoral fraud. Like Putin, Xi too is beginning to see American conspiracies everywhere to export "color revolutions" to authoritarian regimes. His fear seems to be confirmed by the brief attempt to export Spring to China with the – ephemeral – protest movement called the Jasmine Revolution. The Communist Party faces a decisive test, a matter of life and death, according to Xi. Shortly after winning the nomination as party secretary and president of the republic, his campaign against corruption becomes a stepping stone towards the acquisition of an unprecedented power since the days of Mao. Xi liquidates other top bosses, including top military and police leaders. Always accusing them of stealing. It vanquishes opposing factions, but it probably also carries out a real moral cleansing. Thus it gains huge popularity among the citizens.

His rhetoric has nothing to envy to the populism, nationalism and sovereignty that were advancing in those years in the West: indeed, in many ways Xi preceded those trends. His rhetoric alternates between references to Maoism and emulation of America. It is he who systematically uses the image of the Chinese Dream, modeled on the American Dream. However, he does not hesitate to dust off Mao's revolutionary myths such as the Long March (the epic of partisan warfare), for example when he invites the Chinese to face the trade dispute with the United States as a test of resistance. He asks the party leaders to be "commander and warrior". It invokes "Mao's original aspirations", uses terms such as "rebirth and regeneration", evokes a collective catharsis from which to emerge strengthened, more united and powerful than ever.

Another test case for Xi is the Hong Kong issue. Also in this case his personal biography is a precious key to deciphering his thoughts and actions. Again the father figure appears. After Mao's death and Xi Zhongxun's rehabilitation, the father of the current chairman is recovered in a command function in the southern province of Guangdong. Between 1978 and 1980, Father Xi was at the forefront of the experiment of the transition to capitalism that was started in that region. He also has to deal with the flight of Chinese to Hong Kong: political dissidents or economic emigrants looking for work on the island still administered by the British. Xi father is one of the communist leaders who pursue a twofold objective: to hook the richest economies to give the Chinese people a future; while ensuring China's national unity and territorial integrity. Xi Jinping paid implicit homage to his father's memory when he visited Hong Kong in 2017, and there proclaimed his firm intention to fight any separatist temptations.

Popular revolts are a threat to the unity of the nation: this is a recurring theme in the history textbooks on which the younger generations are trained. The beginning of Chinese greatness and the very name of the country are made to coincide with the emperor Qin (pronounced *cin*) Shi Huang who in 221 BC subjugated rival factions and imposed the first unity. Popular protests, on the other hand, since ancient history are often harbingers of chaos, political crises, and mark the end of dynasties. "The disintegration," says historian Arthur Waldron of the University of Pennsylvania, "begins at the periphery of the empire, then grows into adjacent territories, eventually threatening the central seat of power. This is how the Tang dynasty fell in the 10th century, mortally wounded by military disturbances far from the capital» (quoted by Gordon Chang, *Hong Kong May Topple Communism* , in «The Wall Street Journal», September 25, 2019). Another historical moment that is studied as a crucial chapter for the beginning of Chinese decadence is the Taiping revolt in the mid-nineteenth century. This too begins on the periphery, in a southern area not far from Hong Kong. It will lead to 20 million deaths and will be the beginning of the end for the Qing dynasty, the last of the Celestial Empire, destined to fall in 1912.

Hong Kong is a symbolic place for another painful chapter in national history: that island becomes British after the first Opium War (1839-1842). The conflict – which I described in detail in my book *When Our Story Begins*

– is unleashed by the British to defend their "right" to engage in large-scale drug trafficking; they win it and force the Celestial Empire to open its ports, giving up protectionism even against opium. It is there that the Century of Humiliations begins, as it is called in the schools of the People's Republic. For Xi, the Hong Kong uprising in 2019 sets off all the alarm bells: that island is a concentrate of historical, personal and national memories. Whether or not he believes in the American conspiracy theories behind the street protests, whether he is genuinely frightened by fears of contagion or whether he cynically manipulates certain national symbols, it is difficult to know. One of the limitations of the authoritarian regime is this: the subordinates, those who have to inform the top leader about the reasons for the events shaking the former British colony, tend to confirm what he wants to hear.

In a major speech at the Communist Party's central school on September 3, 2019, Xi lists Hong Kong, Macao and Taiwan as the main obstacles to realizing his Chinese Dream. The distrust of what is happening in Hong Kong can only be fueled by the behavior of certain magnates of local capitalism. The richest tycoon on the island, head of a dynasty that was already thriving under the British, is 91-year-old Li Ka-shing. In 2019, his financial conglomerate Hutchison now had only 3 percent of its business in Hong Kong, 54 percent in Europe, 10 percent in Canada. Pushing him towards that diversification abroad is an implicit sense of insecurity: entrepreneurs in China do not enjoy the same protections offered by the rule of law in the West; the more Hong Kong slides towards the control of the mother country, the less solid are its guarantees.

The behavior of billionaires like Li Ka-shing parallels the evolution of the younger generation whose cosmopolitan identity borders on provocation, when seen through Xi's eyes. A Hong Kong University survey carried out in June 2019 indicates that among the 18-29 age group, those who identify themselves as "Hong Kong citizens rather than Chinese" have increased from 40 percent to 90 percent in a decade . These are signs of defiance that risk confirming Xi's theorem of separatism. There is no worse offense than that caused by some young demonstrators when they displayed the English flags: anyone who misses the Western master is a traitor, an anti-patriot. However, he is reassured by the fact that the majority of Chinese in the People's Republic do not sympathize with the protests in Hong Kong. Furthermore, in the economic sphere the specific weight of the island has decreased compared to the rest of the country.

Communist China's nationalism is a cornerstone of Xi's ideology. In this the leader does nothing but update and relaunch a tradition inaugurated by Mao. From the first years of school, the Chinese population is trained on history textbooks that reconstruct all the abuses of the West, portray America and Europe as hostile powers that have always wanted to degrade China; they attribute to the Communist Party alone the ability to restore national honour. This indoctrination was recounted by Shanghai-based writer Jianan Qian at celebrations marking the 70th anniversary of the revolution on October 1, 2019.

The first thing to remember about Chinese patriotism is that it is born out of conflict. Unlike democratic countries where people vote to choose their leaders, the Communist Party of China asserted its legitimacy in the Sino-Japanese War. The party led the Chinese people to the final victory to overthrow "the rule of imperialism, feudalism, bureaucratic capitalism" and "founded the People's Republic of China", as stated in the preamble of the Constitution. Consequently, loving the state means supporting the party. "Without the Communist Party there would be no New China" as the famous red song goes. And patriotism was also born of shame. As children we learned that the Qing imperial government had been so weak that it signed several unfair treaties with Western and Japanese colonizers during the 19th century. We learned that even after the fall of the Empire in 1911, the new government, dominated by warlords, was so corrupt that it allowed the Japanese to occupy the Shandong region after World War I. We learned that millions of our countrymen had been killed during the Sino-Japanese War. We internalized the trauma of the Nanking massacre in 1937-38. ... After years of schooling every Chinese retains a wardrobe of collective enemies: Western nations and Japan. (Jianan Qian, *The Making of a Chinese Patriot*, in The New York Times, Sept. 28, 2019.)

Xi has reinforced nationalist propaganda in his messages. The idea that the West nurtures an ancient hostility towards China, that America and Europe are nostalgic for the times when they could humiliate it with impunity, is part of the narrative of a recovery led by the Communist Party. In this sense, the trade war is explained as the confirmation that the Americans do not tolerate China's new status as an economic superpower, and would do anything to push it back into a condition of inferiority. When the United States calls for structural reforms during bilateral negotiations, such as the abandonment of subsidies to state-owned companies, an end to discrimination against foreign companies, new protections of intellectual property, for Xi it is clear what their real goal is : to weaken the commanding power of the Communist Party over the economy which is the very nature of the system. When Washington demands reciprocity and wants the rules to be applied impartially and transparently by local courts, it essentially aims to establish a rule of law in China which is antithetical to communist power: the party, the true interpreter of the national interest, must dictate the behavior of the courts.

Another useful piece to understand Xi's personality is the intellectual climate that accompanies his rise. An increasingly authoritative circle of Chinese experts is suffering from a sort of "Bismarck syndrome". He interprets the current US-China tension in light of what happened when the chancellor of the Second Reich accomplished German unification, made Germany an empire, and governed the early stages of Britain's economic run-up. Germany's legitimate aspiration at the end of the nineteenth century to be an industrial superpower, to have "living space and a place in the sun", would have been opposed by the old dominant peoples such as the English and French, not to counter a real danger of oppression, but out of selfishness and envy. The narrative on an incompatibility of values between the Second Reich and its neighbors, i.e. the idea that it was necessary to stop an authoritarian power in the name of the more liberal principles in vogue in London, would have been an ex post rationalization to give a patina of nobility to *a* conflict purely geopolitical, a rivalry between powers. From this point of view, Xi sees our reservations about Chinese authoritarianism as specious, diversions that hide our true motivation. The current climate of a new cold war would be yet another proof of the selfishness of the West, which does not admit the rise of a power as different from itself as China. Everything else is lies: our criticisms of human rights or the environment, our denunciations of the Chinese arms race, our protectionism. Behind it there would be only America's claim to cling to its supremacy, to defend positions of supremacy and privilege.

This reading of the present is also consistent with the metaphor of the "Thucydides trap" repeatedly evoked by Xi himself. One of the "organic" political thinkers of the Chinese president is Yan Xuetong, a professor at

Tsinghua University in Beijing. His most cited book has been translated into English: *Leadership and the Rise of Great Powers* (Princeton University Press, 2019). Yan does not embrace the official rhetoric – the one that his president went to recite in front of the globalist audience of the World Economic Forum in Davos – that is, the idea that the rise of China brings benefits for everyone. To that exportable version, Yan prefers a more realistic and hard-line view of international affairs: the rise of a power like China inevitably comes at the expense of America. Yan also openly calls for a more aggressive military profile from his country. Already in an interview with the "New York Times" on February 9, 2016, he urged Xi Jinping to emulate Vladimir Putin in his military expansion in the Middle East, that is, he advised to "offer military aid to friendly countries to ensure strategic cooperation and political support".

These are different words from the traditional rhetoric which presented us with Chinese expansion as a harmless, benevolent phenomenon under the banner of harmony among peoples. After all, the US-China bipolarity is already evident in the trends in arms spending. The United States remains the first nation in the world in terms of defense budget. The latest official data refers to 2018 (source Sipri) and estimates US military spending at 650 billion dollars. In the same year, Chinese expenditure reached 250 billion dollars, i.e. "only" 38.5 percent of American spending. Assuming that the Chinese figure is reliable, however, this photograph is static and does not capture the very different dynamics: in the decade 2009-2018, American spending decreased by 17 percent while that of China increased by 83 percent. Also in this field it is clear where the trajectories point: towards overtaking.

Other considerations about these numbers are important. First, America is forced to disperse its military might in areas that the Chinese military cares little about (at least for now), such as Europe; consequently the budget for armaments is spent in a less efficient way because it is "spread" to the four corners of the planet. China has given itself a more precise initial objective: to maximize the costs of an American intervention in the Far East. Equipping itself with lighter but deadly armaments, the "asymmetric wars" that Beijing is simulating are more like the tactics of the guerrillas or the mini-fleets with which Iran sows fear in the Persian Gulf. In the event of a Chinese attack on

Taiwan, for example, Americans may realize that proximity to China's coast gives the People's Liberation Army an insurmountable advantage, and that US aircraft carriers are behemoths built to fight past wars. Attacked by swarms of drones and mini-submarines, as well as by hackers, US fleets could prove to be very expensive but bankruptcy investments. Finally, it is interesting to note that while there is still a considerable distance in military budget between the United States and China, greater distances separate all other nations from China. In other words, this is a classic bipolar situation. Everyone else will eventually be forced to choose sides. Just like during the First Cold War. Those who have not yet decided "what they will do when they grow up", i.e. the European Union, risk paying heavy prices in terms of loss of autonomy. One way or the other.

What I have called the "Bismarck syndrome" can perhaps be declined in several ways. The old European powers like England and France did not understand – or did not want to understand – the legitimate ambitions of a newcomer like Germany, and closed themselves in an arrogant defense. But the Second Reich in turn did not feel the level of fear it was instilling in its neighbours. Errors and underestimations were reciprocal, until the two world wars. We can say the same thing about China too. In part, it is we who do not understand its legitimate aspirations, out of selfishness, out of ignorance, because we don't study it enough. But even the rulers of Beijing have shown a disconcerting inability to decipher what is happening in the West.

The impact of globalization over the past quarter century has two faces. The Chinese boom saved 750 million people from hunger and lifted them out of poverty, an extraordinarily positive phenomenon. At the same time it has dismantled pieces of Western economies; and those American or European elites who have accumulated profits on globalization have lost interest in the impoverishment of large sections of fellow citizens. All of this was to produce a political backlash. China did not foresee this, and still only partially understands it. Or perhaps Xi Jinping is guided by his analysis of the weakness of Western liberal democracies. He sees that there are two Americas increasingly incapable of speaking and listening to each other, separated by geographical and racial, religious, values and social fault lines. He despises a country so divided, governed by a political system that seems to have gone mad. From Xi's point of view, the institution of impeachment is the supreme proof of weakness: a political system that provides for the deposition of the leader is the antithesis of decision-making, governance and unity of command. Xi perhaps thinks that the real long-term weakness is the irremediable fragmentation within American society and between the people and the elite: it is not befitting the management of an empire. Trump has nothing to do with it, because Xi despised Obama and Clinton even more.

History is full of misunderstandings, misunderstandings, underestimations. Richard Nixon's visit to Mao Zedong, the landing of Air Force One in Beijing on February 21, 1972 after a quarter of a century without diplomatic relations, was not immediately understood. In the long run, that historical turning point would have generated Deng Xiaoping and his market reforms, but also the Tiananmen Square massacre; China's entry into the WTO and its take-off towards prosperity but also the impoverishment of the western middle class and populism. Today that whole phase is probably closing before our eyes; we are heading towards something else. Not everything starts with Trump nor is it his fault. The rules of the game of globalization, established between 1999 and 2001, therefore tailor-made for a then very poor China, are now tight for a West in difficulty. The trade war, which in the media narrative is blamed on America, was actually started - and won hands down - by China.

The dispute over tariffs is a concentration of misunderstandings, misunderstandings, half-truths. Let's take one of the many temporary and constantly evolving episodes in that escalation of customs duties accompanied by temporary truces and armistices. The date is September 1, 2019. The list of Chinese products on which the new 15 percent duties in the United States was triggered that day is 114 pages long. From televisions to shoes to sporting goods, the range covers 112 billion in annual imports. Tariffs are a weapon (not the only one) that Trump uses in his diplomacy: an arsenal with which he wants to redesign the global balance of forces, the rules of the game in the global economy. Surprisingly, a winner of the first "round" is the American financial market: Wall Street and the dollar are at their highest that day. When the going gets tough, when uncertainty increases, capital from all over the world

(Chinese included) still tends to take refuge in the United States. The list of losers sees in the lead the economies that depend most on exports: Germany, China, Italy, plus many emerging countries.

With the new tariffs in force since September 1, the share of taxed products that are destined for the American customer jumps from 30 to 70 percent. The average tax-customs burden on goods imported into America from China rose from 3 percent in 2017 to 24 percent. Which in reality is barely enough to "even out" the level of duties that were already applied by Beijing on goods made in the USA, long before the tug of war between the two governments began. This is not a minor detail, even if it is almost always overlooked in the West, where a critical attitude towards Trump prevails. What the media define as super tariffs when America adopts them are actually the normal tariffs that Beijing has been using for many years, by virtue of the facilitated rules that were negotiated when China was an underdeveloped nation, and ran the risk of succumbing in competition with we. The chorus of criticisms of Trump's tariffs highlights an American weakness that was known: over the last quarter of a century several US multinationals have built a logistics chain spread over several continents, with production bases delocalized in China and other Asian countries. The tariffs have upset the economic calculations that were at the basis of that logistic chain. Some multinationals have begun to recognize that we have entered a new phase of globalization, and have embarked on alternative plans to reduce their dependence on China. But these are not plans that are implemented in a few months.

In the confrontation between the two American and Chinese protectionisms, the United States enjoys the stronger bargaining position in the long run. First of all due to the trade imbalance itself which is at the origin of the tension: a country that exports to another country five times as much as it imports is obviously more vulnerable than the other to tariffs. Moreover, the ability to retaliate "an eye for an eye, duty for duty" is limited by the fact that China already started with much higher levels of customs duties.

The word "autarchy" evokes, for some generations, the stories of our parents or grandparents about Mussolini's Italy and a mediocre substitute for coffee or other imported goods. The term *import substitution* , which is used in economics textbooks, has a more glamorous sound . The essence is that: to replace an imported product with one that is manufactured in one's own national territory and therefore creates jobs and wealth for our fellow citizens. *Import substitution* policies have redistributive implications. If so far consumers have bought foreign products in a number of sectors, it is generally because they are of better quality, or more often because they are cheaper. It's the "China discount" we've all enjoyed as shoppers going grocery shopping for the last 20 years. The replacement, therefore, is paid for by the consumer, who must accept a premium to "buy American." In some cases – labour-intensive industries such as textiles, clothing, footwear – substitution is almost impossible: many products no longer exist on the national territory. In other cases, bringing factories back to America means hiring more robots than humans. While waiting for companies to convince themselves that autarky is lasting, and to have the advantage of reinvesting in the construction of factories on the national territory, those products will continue to be imported.

Who pays the duty, say 20 percent? The hope of those who impose it is that it will be paid by the exporter: by reducing its profits, or possibly the wages of Chinese workers. But it may be that those wages are so low that they are not compressible. It may be that the exporting company is not willing to drastically reduce its profit margins. Several US multinationals are trying to relocate factories from China to Vietnam, Bangladesh, Cambodia and other countries not affected by the tariffs. But Vietnam, despite being one of Southeast Asia's new tigers, has a population that is one-tenth the size of China and a much smaller economy. It cannot replace the neighbor. Surely these relocations don't happen overnight. It took China thirty years to become a reliable supplier by investing in very modern logistics infrastructure. The market knows how to respond to changes in costs, but it takes time to make such massive conversions. Therefore, the short-term US costs cannot be ignored.

The economic escalation of the Second Cold War seems to know no bounds, every sector becomes a virtual battlefield, after trade duties and the embargo on technologies, new variants aim to raise walls even in the financial markets. It was at the end of September 2019 that the Trump administration leaked the possibility of delisting Chinese companies that are listed on American stock exchanges. In parallel, bans on buying securities in China for US institutional investors such as pension funds could come into effect. There are 156 Chinese companies listed on American stock exchanges, with a total capitalization of 1.2 trillion dollars. These include the three giants of the digital economy Alibaba, Baidu and Tencent. There are also 11 state-owned companies in the list of listed companies. The offensive that America is studying comes from afar and is not strictly linked to the trade war.

One of the Republican exponents who deals with Chinese affairs, Florida Senator Marco Rubio, has been campaigning for years to reduce Beijing's access to the American capital market. Already under the Obama administration the alarm was sounded about the opacity of the financial statements of Chinese companies. The certification of their accounts by *auditing firms* is sometimes covered by state secrecy, especially if they are public or defense-related entities. In 2015, the Chinese branches of the major auditing and certification companies - Deloitte, Ernst & Young, Kpmg, PwC - had negotiated and paid fines to the Securities and Exchange Commission (the US financial market supervisory body) for refusing to provide information on the financial statements of listed Chinese companies.

For some time, therefore, there has been concern in the American establishment about the asymmetry of relations, the possibility for China to use the New York market to raise capital without submitting to the rules of local competitors. China's growth on the stock exchange has been spectacular: in 2019 it overtook America for the number of listed companies appearing in the "Fortune 500" ranking: Chinese reached 129 against 121 Americans. But delisting them from the price lists will not be easy, precisely by virtue of the rule of law that attracts Chinese capitalists to America. In fact, they will have ample power of appeal, and independent tribunals will decide. All guarantees that do not exist in Beijing for foreign investors. The capital raised by listing on American stock exchanges can go to finance programs such as "Made in China 2025" with which China aims to oust the United States from technological primacy.

Always in the logic of "not financing the enemy", another move being studied in Washington would block the investments of public pension funds in Chinese companies. Many pension funds automatically link the composition of their portfolios to international indices; and the weight of Chinese stock exchanges has been increasing for many years within the category of emerging countries. The bulletin of the most recent hostilities includes a sector other than finance but related: naval transport. Washington has put three Chinese shipowners on a blacklist of sanctionable companies, two of which belong to Cosco, which is the largest shipping company in the world. Cosco is controlled by the state and most of China's oil supply depends on it. The subsidiaries affected by the US sanction own 50 tankers. The American accusation is of having violated the embargo on Iran's oil supplies. The link with finance lies in the so-called "extraterritoriality" of the American sanctions. Any company that needs to use dollars - the dominant currency in commercial transactions - finds itself in the purview of American punishment. In the case of the Cosco subsidiaries, energy brokers and intermediaries around the world have had to look for replacements for those vessels, as no one wants to be "blacklisted", banned from global financial circuits.

The story of Cosco and its supertankers is emblematic because it calls into question another of the terrains on which the America-China challenge is played out: energy. This fact must be included in their balance of power: America, for the first time in seventy-five years, has recently returned to exporting oil and gas. First there was the technological revolution of *fracking and horizontal drilling* , which generated the boom in the extraction of fossil energies; then Trumpian deregulation. The repercussions of the manufacturing boom extend to geoeconomics and geopolitics. America is now firmly in the leading trio of energy powers, with Saudi Arabia and Russia; no longer imports a single drop of oil from the Persian Gulf; on the contrary, it puts itself in direct competition on the markets. While China remains heavily dependent on imported energy. And as long as the Strait of Malacca is manned by US military fleets, it is a kind of jugular vein where the United States could strangle the adversary in case of armed conflict. China would theoretically have large reserves of *shale* gas, but it lacks the technologies and above all the water to extract them.

When one wonders about the future of the US-China challenge, and wonders if we are in the transition phase from the American century to a Chinese century, in evaluating the balance of forces between the two superpowers one must take into account the factor of natural resources, as well as of its reflections on vulnerability related to climate change. Due to the greater density of its population, the ongoing desertification processes, the scarcity of arable land and water reserves, China has a long-term environmental handicap.

Who will govern the next crisis, if a global economic recession crosses the scenario of the new cold war? We don't know when or how or where it will break out, but there will be a crisis. The economy has its seasonal cycles. The American recovery that began in the summer of 2009 was the longest since the mid-nineteenth century. Chinese growth has not stopped since 2003, when it ran into the Sars epidemic: it is unlikely that China invented perpetual motion. The problem is that the next global crisis – whatever its place of origin and triggering cause – will be the first of the sovereign era. The shock of 2008 was managed by leaders like Barack Obama, Hu Jintao, Gordon Brown, Mario Draghi: personalities who now belong to another universe, with a different vision of the world. Xi has worked to build the premises for a confrontation, not only with his protectionism, with his state dirigisme, with military reinforcement and geopolitical expansionism, but openly theorizing for many years that his authoritarian political system is more effective than ours shattered liberal democracies. If he gets into trouble, he certainly won't want to lose face. And in this he looks a lot like the president of the United States.

Perhaps this too is an indication of the "China syndrome" that is gripping Americans, for better or for worse. There is an obsessive aspect to the attention paid to the rival superpower. The two best documentaries recently released in American theaters concern China. The first is called *American Factory* and is a true story that has its epicenter in Dayton, Ohio. We are in the industrial Midwest that elected Trump, the Rust Belt or "rust belt": so called because most of the factories are "rusty", in decline due to Asian competition. One of these is closed by General Motors, which puts thousands of employees and their families in crisis. A white knight arrives, a savior: he is Chinese. An industrialist who produces glass for cars takes over the abandoned factory and hires two thousand workers. Half the previous salary. But still better than unemployment. The film is the accurate and balanced story of an industrial experiment which is also the clash between two cultures. One of the tragicomic moments is the visit of a delegation of American workers to the Chinese parent company. They are appalled when they see the "military" maneuvers to which their Chinese colleagues undergo in the morning before starting their work shifts: in a show of discipline, they move together like small regiments going to the parade under shouted orders from the officers. The inverted mirror of this culture shock is the speech that a Chinese master builder makes to his colleagues to explain to them that they cannot harshly scold American workers when they make some mistakes: «You see, they have accustomed them differently from us since they were children, at school . No one ever told them they were wrong. They were always pampered and encouraged, at most the teacher would tell them: you can do better. They are like donkeys, they must be stroked in the direction of the hair».

The other documentary deals with a more tragic subject. *One Child Nation* is a journey inside the most gigantic birth control experiment in the history of mankind. The one-child policy was adopted in 1979 and was applied – with modifications – until a few years ago. The author of the documentary is a 30-year-old Chinese woman who now lives in the United States. When he explores his home country, accumulating interviews and testimonies, he manages to have an objective look. Many stories are repulsive. Especially in the countryside, where peasant families considered their children a productive resource to fight hunger and were used to having numerous offspring, the one-child policy was applied with ruthless methods. Forced abortions. Sterilizations imposed with violence, especially on women. A traffic of fake orphans was born, especially girls, abandoned and put up for sale. The documentary hides nothing of the horrors and sufferings. At the same time, many women who suffered those abuses justify them in hindsight. "It was terrible but necessary" is a phrase that recurs among many interviewees. Today's China would have 350 million more inhabitants. "We would have remained poor forever," say some of these peasant women. No other country has ever managed to defuse the population bomb in such a short time. The comparison with Africa makes us think. Without the one-child policy, perhaps today we would be discussing gigantic waves of migration from China?

A common message about China emerges from the two documentaries: here is a nation, indeed a civilization, which puts the collective interest, the good of the community, before the wishes of individuals. Before making summary judgments, we must carefully observe the reasons for this profound difference between us and them, without blinkers. In the Long March that Xi has in mind, the Chinese's capacity for suffering is an ingredient of final victory. The other ingredient is the division of Westerners: not only the gap between Europe and the United States, but the fact that in liberal democracies the sense of a common destiny seems to have vanished. For many Americans, for many Europeans, the enemy to be brought down is within their own country, it is the leader of the opposing faction, or whoever voted for him. The Second Cold War, like so many wars of the past, will be decided by the "home front".

Don't miss out!

Visit the website below and you can sign up to receive emails whenever Jensen Cox publishes a new book. There's no charge and no obligation.

https://books2read.com/r/B-A-ZNXX-JGVJC

BOOKS 2 READ

Connecting independent readers to independent writers.

Also by Jensen Cox